Facts about Germany

Imprint

Publishers:
Societäts-Verlag, Frankfurt/Main, in collaboration with the German Federal Foreign Office, Berlin

Societäts-Verlag
Concept and chief editor:
Peter Hintereder
Project coordination: Andreas Fiebiger
Editors: Janet Schayan, Dr. Sabine Giehle
Translation: Jeremy Gaines
Art direction and design:
Bruno Boll, Katharina Rudolph
Production: Jörn Roßberg

Societäts-Verlag
Frankenallee 71-81
60327 Frankfurt/Main
Germany
Internet: www.fsd.de
E-mail: tatsachen@fsd.de; facts@fsd.de

Federal Foreign Office
Directorate-General for Culture and Communication
Werderscher Markt 1
10117 Berlin, Germany
Internet: www.auswaertiges-amt.de
E-mail: 613-s@auswaertiges-amt.de

Printing: Werbedruck GmbH Horst Schreckhase, Spangenberg, Printed in Germany 2008

Deadline for copy: December, 2007
ISBN: 978-3-7973-1091-0

"Facts about Germany" appears in the following languages:
Arabic, Chinese, Czech, English, Farsi, French, German, Indonesian, Italian, Japanese, Lithuanian, Polish, Portuguese, Russian, Spanish, Turkish and Ukranian

"Facts about Germany" can be accessed on the Internet in several language versions:
www.facts-about-germany.de

Foreword

DID YOU KNOW THAT GERMANY is the third largest economy in the world? That Germany places in the Top 3 preferred locations for foreign students? Or that Germany is ever more popular as a travel destination? "Facts about Germany" invites you to get to know Germany. It offers exhaustive basic information and numerous points of orientation – designed specially for our foreign readers whose interest in contemporary Germany extends beyond coincidental data to be found in the daily flood of news items.

In 11 wide-ranging chapters, renowned authors focus on the major political, social and economic trends in Germany today. These keynote essays offer a well-structured review of the complexities of current German society and illustrate what models and solutions are being discussed in an age of economic and social change.

Special emphases in the text and key words that are to be found in all chapters together form an ongoing index and thus an additional level of information. The "Facts – compact" pages offer discerning graphic documentation on the key facts and a timeline for the respective topic, along with any number of maps, illustrations and contemporary documents. Cross-links in the body of the text as well as the extensive index at the back facilitate swift and systematic access to information. The expanded, comprehensive range of online offerings round out the content in the printed version, providing in-depth and constantly updated information on Germany in numerous different languages (www.facts-about-germany.de).

The publishers would like to take this opportunity to thank everyone who contributed ideas, insights and encouragement and thus played a constructive part in making this issue of "Facts about Germany" a reality.

1
p. 6 Facts and figures
3
p. 26 Past and present
5
p. 70 Foreign policy
2
p. 14 Federal states
4
p. 50 Political system
6
p. 88 The economy

Contents

Facts on the Internet
www.facts-about-germany.de
The Web site accompanying the book offers you basic insights into Germany in 15 languages, including info-graphics, links and countless images.
You can likewise find more detailed background information and in-depth articles on the Internet, specifically as regards the chapters on: the federal states; Germany past and present; education, science, and research; society; and culture.

1

Facts and figures

Germany has many strong suits: The country is renowned for the quality of its products with the trademark "made in Germany" - and it is also a country with a great lifestyle, highly diverse countryside and open-minded inhabitants. An increasing number of foreign students enjoy the academic climate at Germany's universities. International investors appreciate the know-how and superior training of the workforce. The art and cultural scene is brimming over with a zest for experimentation and surprises. This is true of all 16 federal states and in particular of Berlin, as the capital - the country's political and creative heart.

Federal Republic of Germany

State	Democratic parliamentary federal democracy since 1949
Capital city	Berlin, 3.4 million inhabitants
National flag	Three horizontal stripes in black, red, gold
Emblem	Stylized eagle
Anthem	Third verse of August Heinrich Hoffmann von Fallersleben's "Das Lied der Deutschen" to a melody by Joseph Haydn "Kaiserhymne"
State holiday	October 3, Day of German Unity
Parliament	Bundestag (16th legislative period: 613 MPs)
Time zone	CET/CEST
Currency	Germany is a member of the Eurozone, EUR 1 = 100 cents
Phone dial code	+49
Internet TLD	.de (one of the ten most frequent top-level domains)
Official language	German. German is the mother tongue of 100 million people. German is the mother tongue spoken most frequently in the European Union

Geography

Location	Central Europe
Size	357,021 km^2
Borders	3,757 km
Coastline	2,389 km
Neighboring states	Germany is at the heart of Europe and has nine neighbors: Austria, Belgium, the Czech Republic, Denmark, France, Luxembourg, the Netherlands, Poland, and Switzerland
Highest mountain	Zugspitze 2963 m
Longest rivers	Rhine 865 km, Elbe 700 km, Danube 647 km (in Germany)
Largest cities	Berlin 3.4 million inhabitants, Hamburg (1.8m), Munich (1.3m), Cologne (1.0m), Frankfurt/Main (662,000)

Germany is a federation made up of 16 federal states, each of which has independent if constrained state authority

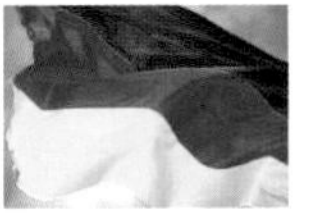

German Federal flag

German Federal emblem

Einigkeit und Recht und Freiheit
für das deutsche Vaterland!
Danach lasst uns alle streben
brüderlich mit Herz und Hand!
Einigkeit und Recht und Freiheit
sind des Glückes Unterpfand.
Blüh im Glanze dieses Glückes,
blühe, deutsches Vaterland!

Text of the German national anthem

Landscape	From the North Sea to the Baltic Sea in the North to the Alps in the South, Germany is structured geographically as follows: the North German lowlands, the Mittelgebirge ridge, the Southwest German subdued mountains and terraced landscape, the South German piedmont and the Bavarian Alps
Climate	Moderate oceanic/continental climatic zone with frequent changes in weather and primarily westerly winds

Population

Inhabitants	With 82.3 million inhabitants (of which 42.0 million are women) Germany has the largest population of any EU member state. Around 7.3 million foreigners live in Germany (8.8 percent of the total population) and of them 1.7 million are Turks
Population density	With 231 inhabitants per square kilometer Germany is one of the most densely populated countries in Europe
Births	On average 1.3 children per woman
Population growth	-0.1%
Age structure	14% less than 15, 20% over 65
Life expectancy	With an average life expectancy of 77 years for men and 82 for women (born in 2006) Germany is above the OECD mean
Urbanization	88% of the population live in cities and conurbations. In Germany, there are 82 cities with a population of over 100,000
Religions	Just under 53 million people profess to be Christians (26m Catholics, 26m Protestants, 900,000 members of the Orthodox churches), 3.3m are Muslims, 230,000 Buddhists, 100,000 Jews, 90,000 Hindus. The Basic Law guarantees freedom of thought, conscience and religion. There is no state religion
Immigration	Since 2005, the new Immigration Act regulates immigration

Political system

Legislation	Bicameral system: in addition to the Bundestag, the Bundesrat (consisting of delegates of the state governments to uphold the states' interests) participates in legislation
State structure	Germany is a federation consisting of 16 federal states, each with its own constitution, parliament and government. The highest state authority is exercised by the federal government. Through the agency of the Bundesrat, the states are represented at the federal level and participate in federal legislation.
Suffrage	Universal, equal and secret suffrage as of 18 years of age (in the case of municipal elections in part as of 16), elections to the Bundestag are held every four years.
Federal President	Prof. Dr. Horst Köhler (CDU) since 2004
Federal Chancellor	Dr. Angela Merkel (CDU) since 2005
Party system	Multi-party system, parties have a special constitutional status, receive state financial support, can only be prohibited by the Federal Constitutional Court

Parties represented in the Bundestag	Social Democratic Party of Germany (SPD), German Christian Democratic Union (CDU), Christian Social Union (CSU), Bündnis 90/Die Grünen (The Greens), Free Democratic Party (FDP), Die Linke (The Left)
Legal system	Germany is a social constitutional state. It is based on the principle of a division of powers and the lawful administration. All organs of state are subject to the constitutional order. The Basic Law guarantees every individual citizen basic and human rights. The Federal Constitutional Court watches over adherence to the Basic Law. All the other organs of state are bound to uphold its rulings

Germany in the world

International cooperation	Germany joins its European and transatlantic partners in championing peace, democracy and human rights the world over. Germany is a member in key European and other international organizations
European Union	The Federal Republic of Germany is a founding member of the European Union (EU). Germany contributes around EUR 22 billion or some 20% of the EU budget and is thus the single largest contributor.
United Nations	Germany has been a full member of the United Nations (UN) since 1973. Germany contributes just under 9 percent of the regular UN budget and is third largest contributor. Germany is a state with a UN seat: Since 1996 Bonn has had the title of "UN City"; 16 UN organizations are based there
Other organizations and alliances	Germany is a member of the NATO defense alliance (since 1955), the Organization of Economic Co-operation and Development (OECD), the Organization for Security and Co-operation in Europe (OSCE), the World Bank and the International Monetary Fund (IMF)
Federal Foreign Office	The Federal Foreign Office, which is headquartered in Berlin and its network of 226 foreign representative offices represents Germany in the world. Germany currently maintains diplomatic relations with 191 countries
Out-of-area operations	The German Armed Forces are committed to nine peace-keeping and humanitarian operations outside the country, all of which are under UN mandates and are carried out in the framework of NATO and the EU. It is one of the countries providing the largest number of troops for international crisis prevention and conflict management missions

Economy

Economic prowess	Germany is the largest economy in the European Union and the third largest in the world. With the highest GDP and the largest number of inhabitants in the EU, Germany is Europe's most important market. Gross Domestic Product comes to EUR 2,423 billion (2007), GNP per capita is EUR 29,455
Export	Germany is the world's leading exporter: the volume of goods exported came to EUR 969 billion in 2007. Key trading partners: France (9.5%), USA (8.7%), Great Britain (7.2%), Italy (6.6%)

Structure	Alongside internationally active corporations, SMEs form the backbone of the German economy. Around 70 % of all employees work in small and medium sized enterprises
Key sectors	Car-making; mechanical, electrical and precision engineering; chemicals; environmental technology; optics; medical technology; biotech and genetic engineering; nanotechnology; aerospace; logistics
Investment magnet	Germany strongly attracts foreign investors. The world's 500 largest corporations are present here, a total of 22,000 foreign companies with a total staff of 2.7 million. Foreign direct investments amounted to US$ 503 billion in 2005.
Infrastructure	Germany has a highly developed infrastructure that is growing dynamically. Its rail network covers 36,000 km, and the road network 230,000 km. The country boasts one of the world's most modern phone and communication networks
Trade fairs	About two thirds of all the world's keynote trade fairs take place in Germany (about 160 international trade fairs)

Research and Development

Patent registrations	Germany is Europe's no. 1 in terms of patent registrations. Together with Japan and the United States, Germany, with its 11,188 triad patent registrations, is among the world's three most innovative countries.
Leading Research institutes	Since 1948, 17 Nobel prizes have been won by Max Planck Society scientists. Likewise internationally renowned: the Fraunhofer-Gesellschaft for applied research and the Helmholtz Association with 15 internationally leading large research institutions

Communications

Freedom of opinion	The Basic Law guarantees the freedom of the press and freedom of opinion
Press	Around 350 daily newspapers with a total circulation of 24 million copies and coverage of 73 % of the population. Largest nationwide subscription newspapers: Süddeutsche Zeitung, Frankfurter Allgemeine Zeitung, Die Welt. With a circulation of 3.6 million, "Bild"-Zeitung has the largest print run in Europe. Deutsche Presse-Agentur (dpa) is the world's fourth largest news agency
Magazines	Der Spiegel, Stern, Focus
Internet	95 % of companies and 61 % of private households have access to the Internet
Radio, TV	Two-prong system: alongside the public (license-based) radio and TV stations (ARD, ZDF) there are private (ad-financed) channels. ZDF is the largest broadcasting station in Europe. Germany's foreign radio station is Deutsche Welle (DW-TV, DW-Radio, DW-world.de and DW-Akademie)

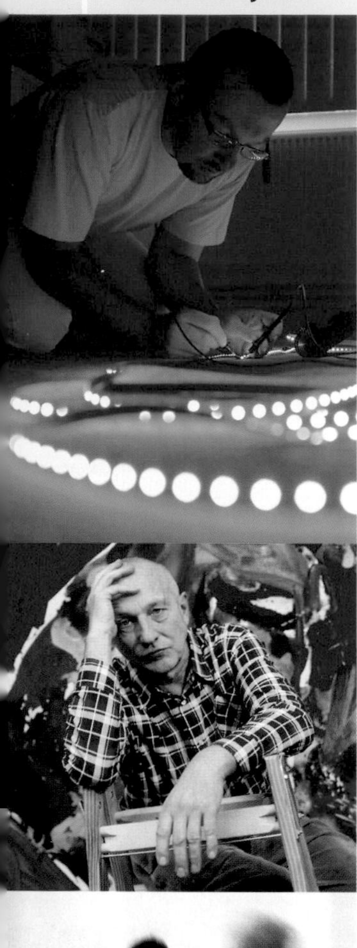

Social system

Social security Germany has an elaborate network of social security systems (pension, health, healthcare and unemployment insurance), financed in equal measure by employees and employers alike

Health Almost all Germany's inhabitants have health insurance (88 % on statutory and just under 12 % in private insurance schemes). Given total outlays on health of 10.7 % of GDP, Germany is well above the OECD average of 9.0 %

Higher education

Higher education There are 383 institutes of higher education in Germany, 103 of them universities, and 176 universities of the applied sciences. 947,000 or 48 % of the total of some two million students are women. Whether tuition fees are charged and the scale difference from one state to the next. In seven states, fees of about EUR 500 per semester are charged for new students, and fees are levied almost everywhere for students who have exceed ten terms or are studying for the second time.

Foreign students 246,000 foreign students are enrolled at German institutes of higher education. After the United States and Great Britain, Germany is thus third most attractive country world-wide for foreign students

Degrees Bachelor's, Master's, Ph.D., State Examination, Diploma, Magister, Promotion

Culture

Tradition German writers, composers and philosophers such as Goethe, Schiller, Bach, Beethoven, Kant and Hegel have strongly influenced cultural epochs and are acclaimed figures the world over

Culture federalism Germany's federal structure and the cultural sovereignty of each federal state ensure that the country boasts a wealth of different cultural institutions and a vibrant cultural scene. Berlin, as the capital city, is a spectacular case in point, with three opera houses, 120 museums, more than 50 theaters and a lively art community that also attracts many young foreign artists

Cultural institutions 5,000 museums (of them 500 art museums), 300 theaters, over 100 musical theaters and opera houses, 130 professional orchestras, 7,500 libraries

Festivals Richard Wagner Festival Bayreuth, Bachfest Leipzig, Berlin International Film Festival (Berlinale), Theatertreffen Berlin, Rock am Ring

Books 95,000 new publications or new editions each year

UNESCO World Heritage Germany features 32 natural and cultural heritage sites protected under the UNESCO World Heritage program

Germany in the Internet

www.deutschland.de
Official portal of the Federal Republic of Germany. It provides access in Arabic, English, French, German, Russian, and Spanish to link lists for all areas of society

www.bundesregierung.de
The comprehensive German federal government Web site, including topical news on government policies (English, French and German)

www.auswaertiges-amt.de
Information on aspects of German foreign policy and addresses of the German missions abroad (Arabic, English, French, German and Spanish)

www.invest-in-germany.de
The Web site of the federal agency Invest in Germany GmbH provides information on Germany as a business hub (in six languages)

www.goethe.de
The Goethe-Institut Web site provides information on language courses and events at the 142 institutes as well as on German culture and society (English and German)

www.ifa.de
The Institut für Auslandsbeziehungen (ifa) offers an overview of topics relating to international cultural exchange (English, German, Portuguese and Spanish)

www.daad.de
The German Academic Exchange Service (DAAD) provides information on funding and exchange programs for students, graduates and scientists (in 22 languages)

www.dw-world.de
German foreign broadcasting station Deutsche Welle (DW) provides a wealth of topical editorial information (in 30 languages)

www.deutschland-tourismus.de
The German National Tourist Board Web site offers a wide range of details on Germany as a holiday destination (English and German)

www.land-der-ideen.de
The "Germany. Land of Ideas" initiative champions Germany as a center and, among other things, runs a special media service (English and German)

www.destatis.de
Web site of the German Federal Statistical Office (English and German)

www.magazine-deutschland.de
Web site of "Deutschland" magazine, with articles on current topics, a service section and a media corner for journalists (in ten languages)

2

Federal states

16 federal states, preceded by more than twice as many kingdoms, principalities and small manorial towns - Germany is a country rich in history. It also has a wide range of different landscapes: sandy beaches on the North and Baltic Seas, and the snow-covered Alps in the south.

The Germans, be they from Bavaria, Saxony, Friesia or Hesse, bring this portrait to life with their dialects and traditions. And it thus comes as no surprise that some 24 million people visit Germany every year. Many of them do not just come once. In their case, the typical German farewell greeting actually comes true: Auf Wiedersehen - See you again!

The Baltic Sea, a vacation paradise: The pier at Sellin on the island of Rügen

The country and the people: A portrait of the 16 federal states

By Klaus Viedebantt

Baden-Württemberg

People in Baden-Württemberg tend not to talk in superlatives, even though the state continually sets records. It is no. 1 in Europe for high-tech, German leader for patent registrations, and famed for its inventors, first and foremost among them Gottlieb Daimler, Carl Benz and Robert Bosch. Today, it is not only Bosch, Daimler, Porsche and Boss, but also mid caps like Fischer (rawl plugs), Stihl (saws) and Würth (screws) that make it the world champion in the export rankings. And when they're not working, they're enjoying the fact that the state boasts more starred cooks than any other. And the local wines are so good as to be an inside tip.

Baden-Württemberg
Capital: **Stuttgart**
Population: **10,739,000**
Surface area in km^2: **35,751.65**
GDP in billion euro: **337.12**
www.baden-wuerttemberg.de

Majestic: Schlossplatz in Stuttgart

Bavaria

The "beer state" of Bavaria also produces fine wine in the Franconia region. The Oktoberfest, Neuschwanstein Castle and the magnificent Alpine scenery attract more foreign tourists than does any other federal state. Yet the slogan "Laptop and Lederhose" demonstrates that there is more to Bavaria than just a lively tradition. Its economy, which is stronger than that of Sweden, boasts global brands such as BMW, Audi, Siemens, MAN and EADS (Airbus). Munich, the state capital, is home to more publishers than any other German city. And even outside Munich, Germany's largest state is thriving: the annual Wagner Festival in Bayreuth is sold out every year, as is the Passion Play in Oberammergau, held once every ten years.

Bavaria
Capital: **Munich**
Population: **12,493,000**
Surface area in km^2: **70,549.19**
GDP in billion euro: **409.48**
www.bayern.de

Romantic: Neuschwanstein Castle, built by Ludwig II, King of Bavaria

Berlin
Capital: **Berlin**
Population: **3,404,000**
Surface area in km²: **891.75**
GDP in billion euro: **80.62**
www.berlin.de

Metropolitan: Potsdamer Platz

Berlin

Once a year, during the Berlinale film festival, the world of the silver screen focuses on Berlin. And the city's inhabitants are used to global interest. After all, the people of Berlin have lived in a capital city since 1458. However, there is also a shady side to the city's history: the rule of the National Socialists and the East German regime, which built a wall right through the heart of the city. Since 1990, Berlin has once again been the undivided capital city. The Museum Island, the Berlin Philharmonic and some 150 theaters ensure the city is unique. The "scholarly capital" boasts 20 institutes of higher education, while also being home to outstanding firms such as Bayer Schering Pharma or Philip Morris. And the ITB, the world's largest tourism fair, highlights the fact that "Berlin is well worth a visit".

Brandenburg
Capital: **Potsdam**
Population: **2,548,000**
Surface area in km²: **29,477.16**
GDP in billion euro: **49.49**
www.brandenburg.de

Historical: Sanssouci Castle

Brandenburg

The densely forested state of Brandenburg surrounds the capital city of Berlin and benefits from the latter's "gin and martini belt". However, with its numerous lakes and forests it also has several trump cards of its own. With the Hohenzollern castles, and in particular Sanssouci Castle, which is included in the UNESCO World Cultural Heritage List, the heart of the Kingdom of Prussia possesses jewels of courtly architecture. Indeed Potsdam is considered one of Germany's most beautiful cities, featuring many architectural highlights. Today the citizens of Brandenburg boast Hollywood productions in the film-producing town of Babelsberg, the European University Viadrina in Frankfurt an der Oder and more than 280 foreign companies, including the German HQ of Ebay.

Bremen
Capital: **Bremen**
Population: **664,000**
Surface area in km²: **404.23**
GDP in billion euro: **25.31**
www.bremen.de

Bremen

The Hanseatic city of Bremen arose through classic maritime trading, in particular with coffee. In the smallest of the federal states (divided into the city of Bremen, and Bremerhaven, some 60 kilometers to the north) the port accounts for every third job. The largest employer, however, is Daimler; and the ports turn around

1,900,000 vehicles annually. The state's cultural life is also influenced by commerce: The Überseemuseum (Overseas Museum) and the Schifffahrtsmuseum (Maritime Museum) attract visitors from all over the country. The merchants' wealth led to the birth of a truly beautiful architectural ensemble: the town hall market square with its Baroque and Renaissance buildings, a tribute to the city's rich history, which began when it was awarded market rights back in 888.

Maritime: Yachts in Bremerhaven

Hamburg

In the city and state of Hamburg it is the port that is the power-house of the economy, though with Airbus, Otto Versand and Beiersdorf also located here, this is not immediately apparent. With its tanker terminals, the port is home to all the major oil-refining companies. For pleasure-seekers, there is the entertainment district of St. Pauli. Yet Hamburg's reputation as a media and science center is of greater importance to its inhabitants. The demand for culture is correspondingly high, and is satisfied by renowned institutes such as the Kunsthalle and just under 40 theaters – including the state opera company with world ballet star John Neumeier. On a national basis Hamburg leads the way when it comes to musicals, which every month bring thousands of visitors thronging to the city.

Hamburg
Capital: **Hamburg**
Population: **1,754,000**
Surface area in km²: **755.16**
GDP in billion euro: **86.15**
www.hamburg.de

Commercial: Speicherstadt in Hamburg

Hesse

Frankfurt am Main is really the only city in Germany that has an international feel to it: The tallest buildings, the largest airport, and the most banks in continental Europe (including the European Central Bank). And the list of superlatives does not stop there; for example, there is the railroad station and the interstate intersection, both of which boast the highest volume of traffic in Germany. All this, despite the fact that the city has a mere 662,000 inhabitants and is not even the capital of Hesse. The elegant city of Wiesbaden has claim to that title. Otherwise the state of Hesse is rather unassuming, with a densely forested upland range of

Hesse
Capital: **Wiesbaden**
Population: **6,075,000**
Surface area in km²: **21,114.72**
GDP in billion euro: **204.28**
www.hessen.de

Worldly: The skyline in Frankfurt/Main

mountains, blessed with Riesling in the Rheingau region, and industry throughout. Opel in Rüsselsheim and VW near Kassel are the major industries, whereas ESA in Darmstadt is responsible for a large share of the European space program.

Mecklenburg-Western Pomerania
Capital: **Schwerin**
Population: **1,694,000**
Surface area in km²: **23,174.17**
GDP in billion euro: **32.51**
www.mecklenburg-vorpommern.de

Imposing: The chalk cliffs on the island of Rügen

Mecklenburg-Western Pomerania

It need not be from outer space, even from a plane Mecklenburg-Western Pomerania, with more than 2,000 lakes, numerous waterways and lush green in-between looks particularly attractive. Together with its 350-kilometer-long Baltic coastline, this Northeastern state is the major venue for water sports enthusiasts in the whole of Central Europe. Small wonder, then, that tourism is the state's main source of income. To make certain this remains the case, around one fifth of the state's total surface area is a nature conservation area. Away from the tourist centers on the coast, shipbuilding and agriculture are otherwise the main sources of employment in this, the country's most thinly populated state. Northern Europe's two oldest universities and several innovative R&D facilities make the state one of the most dynamic regions for high-tech, bio-tech and medi-tech.

Lower Saxony
Capital: **Hanover**
Population: **7,983,000**
Surface area in km²: **47,618.24**
GDP in billion euro: **197.09**
www.niedersachsen.de

Forward-looking: Autostadt in Wolfsburg

Lower Saxony

The state of Lower Saxony has the shipbuilders in Papenburg to thank for its regular global TV appearances – every time the Meyer shipyard pilots a new luxury liner down the narrow River Ems. Yet the major industry in this state, which stretches from the holiday islands on the North Sea coast to the Harz Mountains, is the auto industry, including such names as Volkswagen in Wolfsburg and Continental in Hanover, likewise the hub of TUI's vast operations, one of Europe's largest tourism corporations. Furthermore, twice a year the eyes of the world focus on the state capital: for the Hanover Industrial Trade Fair and CeBIT, the world's largest IT trade fair. Indeed, Hanover has been an international city for a long time now, after all between 1714 and 1837 the rulers of Hanover were also the kings of England.

North Rhine-Westphalia

Nowhere in Germany has more inhabitants, and there is a correspondingly large number of cities: Cologne, with its Gothic cathedral; Bonn, the Federal Republic's first capital city; Düsseldorf, the fashion-conscious state capital; Aachen, under Charlemagne the capital of Europe; Duisburg, with Europe's largest inland port; the business centers of Krefeld and Bielefeld; not to mention Essen and Dortmund, the two major cities in the Ruhr region. They bear witness to the changes in Germany's largest industrial area: Coal mining and steel production area now flanked by bio-chemicals and high-tech. Yet "NRW", as the state is fondly known, not only has Europe's most concentrated research network, but according to UNESCO is alongside New York and Paris one of the world's major cultural regions.

North Rhine-Westphalia
Capital: **Düsseldorf**
Population: **18,029,000**
Surface area in km²: **34,083.52**
GDP in billion euro: **501.71**
www.nordrhein-westfalen.de

Asymmetrical: The Gehry buildings in Düsseldorf

Rhineland-Palatinate

The Rhine valley between Bingen and Koblenz, a gem that is for the most part located in Rhineland-Palatinate, is a key item on the UNESCO World Cultural Heritage List. A center of wine and sparkling wine production, the state is also referred to as "Wineland-Palatinate". Yet from an early date it has been committed to advanced technology, a prime example being chemicals giant BASF. The state has always been innovative, be it on a very long-term basis thanks to Johannes Gutenberg, who invented the first printing press with moveable type in Mainz, or on a more temporary basis with the work of Karl Marx from Trier. Culture and joie-de-vivre are celebrated in all the larger German cities that have Roman history. The 50-plus festivals staged each year attest to this.

Rhineland-Palatinate
Capital: **Mainz**
Population: **4,053,000**
Surface area in km²: **19,847.39**
GDP in billion euro: **100.72**
ww.rheinland-pfalz.de

Touristy: Vineyards on the Rhine

Saarland

Saarbrücken's film festival for German-speaking up-and-coming talent has been the launching pad for many a career, as Franka Potente and Til Schweiger have proved. The state has over the last 200 years changed nationality eight times and the French influence is highly

Saarland
Capital: **Saarbrücken**
Population: **1,043,000**
Surface area in km²: **2,568.65**
GDP in billion euro: **28.01**
www.saarland.de

The World Heritage

Testimony to the past and unique elements of our natural heritage: 32 of the UNESCO-selected monuments to our World Cultural and Natural Heritage are in Germany

1. **Bremen**
   Town Hall and Statue of Roland
2. **Quedlinburg**
   Collegiate Church, Castle and Old Town
3. **Essen**
   "Zollverein" coal mines and industrial complex
4. **Aachen**
   Cathedral and Palatinate Chapel
5. **Cologne**
   High Gothic Cathedral
6. **Brühl**
   Castles of Augustusburg and Falkenlust
7. **Upper Middle Rhine Valley**
   Beautiful and highly diversified cultural landscape
8. **Trier**
   Roman monuments, Cathedral of St. Peter and Church of Our Lady
9. **Messel Pit nr. Darmstadt**
   Fossil site with a wealth of Eocene finds
10. **Lorsch**
   Monumental entrance to the former Benedictine Abbey and the ruins of the Altenmünster monastery
11. **Völklingen**
   Völklinger Hütte ironworks
12. **Speyer**
   Romanesque Imperial Cathedral
13. **Bamberg**
   Old Town of the Bishopric and Imperial City on the banks of the River Regnitz
14. **Regensburg**
   Historic old town
15. **Maulbronn**
   Cistercian monastery complex
16. **Reichenau**
   Monastery island on Lake Constance

Bremen
The statue of Roland in front of the Town Hall is the town's landmark

Quedlinburg
The Old Town is one of the largest standing monuments in Germany

Essen
The "Ruhr Region's Eiffel Tower": The Zollverein coal mine was founded around 1850 and is an industrial and architectural monument

Aachen
Contemporaries considered Charlemagne's Palatinate Chapel a "marvel of architecture"

Upper Middle Rhine Valley
The valley between Bingen, Rüdesheim and Koblenz is considered the epitome of the Romantic banks of the Rhine

Völklingen
The Völklinger Hütte ironworks stands for a century-long history of labor and steel-making

Maulbronn
The monastery is the best preserved Medieval monastery complex North of the Alps

Reichenau
The monastery island attests to the key role Benedictine monasteries played in Medieval times

1 3 4 5 6 7 8 9 10 11 12 15 16 21

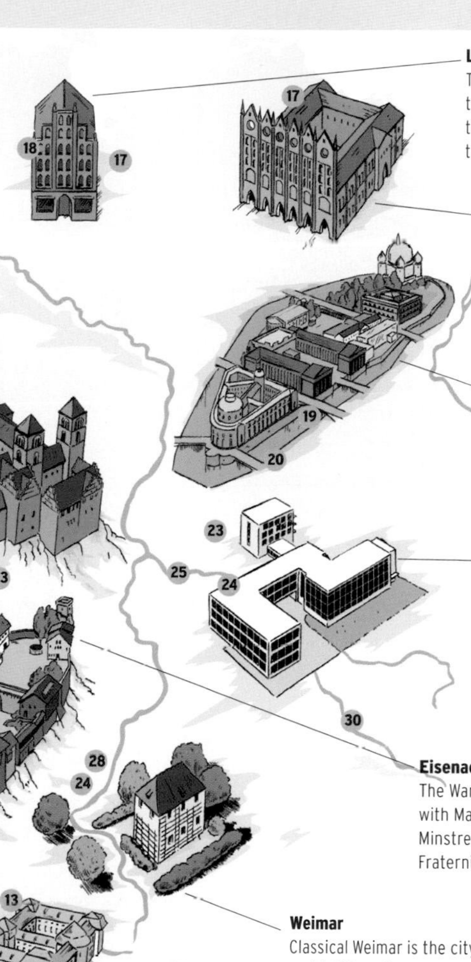

Lübeck
The Medieval heart of the town is exemplary for the Hanseatic cities along the coast of the Baltic Sea

Stralsund and Wismar
Elaborately decorated merchants' homes shape the face of these two Baltic towns

Berlin
An island of culture is formed by the unique ensemble of buildings on the Museum Island

Dessau
Walter Gropius' "Academy of Design" was sought out by many avant-garde architects as the place of learning

Eisenach
The Wartburg is associated with Martin Luther, The Minstrels War, and the Dueling Fraternity Festival

Weimar
Classical Weimar is the city of Goethe and Schiller, of Herder and Wieland

Würzburg
The Residence of the Lord Bishops is considered the jewel of South German Baroque

Limes
Together with Hadrian's Wall, the German section of the defensive wall of the Roman Empire, forms a cross-border World Heritage Site

Steingaden
The Church of "Wies" at the foot of the Alps is one of the most perfect examples of Bavarian Rococo art

www.unesco.de

17 Stralsund and Wismar
The Old Towns of both Hanseatic cities

18 Lübeck
Old Town with the Town Hall, Fortified Monastery, Holsten Gate and Salt Silos

19 Berlin
Museum Island with the Pergamon Museum and the Nationalgalerie

20 Potsdam and Berlin
Palaces and parks in Potsdam's Sanssouci district and Berlin

21 Hildesheim
Romanesque St. Michael's Church and St. Mary's Cathedral

22 Goslar
Old Town and historical Rammelsberg silver mines

23 Wittenberg and Eisleben
Luther Memorials including the house where he was born

24 Dessau and Weimar
The Bauhaus School of Architecture and its sites

25 Dessau-Wörlitz
Garden Kingdom of the Prince of Anhalt-Dessau

26 Bad Muskau
German/Polish cultural heritage site: Muskau Park/Park Muzakowski

27 Eisenach
Wartburg Castle, symbol of German unity

28 Weimar
Unique testimony to Classical Weimar

29 Würzburg
Würzburg Residence, including the marvelous Court Gardens

30 Dresden
Elbe Valley between Übigau Castle and the Elbe Isle in the Southeast

31 Roman Limes in Germany
550 kilometers long, the longest monument on the ground in Europe

32 Steingaden
Church of "Wies"

evident. Mining is now no longer the key industry, with steel and car-making competing with IT for the number one slot. The steel industry bequeathed a fascinating attraction: Völklingen Ironworks, which is included in the UNESCO World Cultural Heritage List. The state's most famous name, however, has to be that of Villeroy & Boch, a global player in the porcelain market.

Picturesque: The "Saarschleife"

Saxony
Capital: **Dresden**
Population: **4,250,000**
Surface area in km²: **18,413.91**
GDP in billion euro: **88.71**
www.sachsen.de

Splendid: The banks of the Elbe near Dresden

Saxony

Meissen may well be a small town but, thanks to its porcelain, is as well known as the state capital Dresden and Leipzig, the trade-fair city. The Free State is one of the most dynamic economic regions in East Germany, in particular in IT; precision watch-making and car-making are typical of this new gearing, symbolized by the restored Frauenkirche in Dresden's Baroque center. As in the past, Saxony's culture is highly influential in the world of music, represented by the Semper opera house in Dresden and the almost 800-year old Thomaner Choir in Leipzig, where Johann Sebastian Bach was once a cantor. Is he the greatest Saxon ever? Bach at least has a serious rival – in the person of Richard Wagner.

Saxony-Anhalt
Capital: **Magdeburg**
Population: **2,442,000**
Surface area in km²: **20,445.26**
GDP in billion euro: **50.14**
www.sachsen-anhalt.de

Saxony-Anhalt

In honor of its most famous former inhabitant, Georg Friedrich Handel, every year Halle stages a major festival. However, the composer plays second fiddle to Martin Luther, the reformer from Eisleben who transformed the Christian world. As such the town of Wittenberg is one of the most popular tourist spots in a state that boasts a wealth of castles but is also renowned for its chemicals industry. Since reunification, the state has been highly successful in attracting investors. Today, Total maintains a refinery in Leuna, Dow Chemical has a production facility in Schkopau, as does Bayer in Bitterfeld. While nature enthusiasts are drawn to the 1141-meter high Brocken mountain, with its myth-shrouded peak: on the eve of every May 1st witches congregate here to dance.

Central: The Handel monument in Halle

Schleswig-Holstein

The most feared mythical figure in Schleswig-Holstein is "Blanker Hans", who stands for the destructive forces of the sea. After all, the most northern of the federal states is bordered by two seas, the North Sea and the Baltic Sea. Since time immemorial, ship-building and fishing have been correspondingly important, with two thirds of the German fishing fleet registered here. Nowadays, however, the main source of income is tourism and agriculture. The North Sea island of Sylt is a fashionable holiday destination. Kiel, the state capital and the Hanseatic city of Lübeck, now immortal thanks to Thomas Mann, vie for the status of most important city. Alongside Puttgarden they are the state's most important ferry ports for the Scandinavia routes. Parallel to developments in Eastern Europe the state also benefits from the Baltic Sea economic region.

Schleswig-Holstein
Capital: **Kiel**
Population: **2,834,000**
Surface area in km²: **15,763.18**
GDP in billion euro: **69.86**
www.schleswig-holstein.de

Idyllic: The broad skies over Schleswig-Holstein

Thuringia

The mountains in the Thuringian Forest provide a backdrop for one of Germany's most beautiful trails, the 160-kilometer long Rennsteig. It is just as much a trademark of the state as its long thin sausages, the historic Wartburg and the Weimar poets Goethe and Schiller. However, Thuringia not only has a culinary and literary tradition, it was always a state of researchers. Zeiss and Schott founded the modern optics industry in Jena; alongside the carmaker Opel and turbine manufacturer Rolls-Royce, Jenoptik is nowadays one of the most important companies there. Erfurt, the state capital, is proud of the flourishing bio- and solar technology there, in addition to the excellent educational opportunities offered by four institutes of higher education. ●

Thuringia
Capital: **Erfurt**
Population: **2,311,000**
Surface area in km²: **16,172.14**
GDP in billion euro: **45.99**
www.thueringen.de

Klaus Viedebantt
The journalist was head of section at the "Zeit" and "FAZ" newspapers and has written numerous travel guides.

Past and present

Germany's path to a liberal constitutional democracy and a functioning parliamentary system involved many historical ruptures: particularism in the early years of the Modern age, the failure of the March Revolution and the Weimar Republic through to the "flaw in history" caused by National Socialism.

Unity and liberty, key concepts since the 19th century, also occupied Germans during the nation's division after the Second World War. Not until reunification in 1990 was the "German issue" resolved.

Peaceful Revolution: On November 9, 1989 the Berlin Wall, the symbol of a divided Germany, comes down

Farewell to the German question – Looking back at the long journey West

By Heinrich August Winkler

IT EXISTED FOR 184 YEARS, the German Question. It arose on August 6, 1806 when Franz II, the last Emperor of the Holy Roman Empire of the German Nation, bowed down to an ultimatum from Napoleon, laid down his crown, relieved the Estates of their duties and thereby dissolved the "Old Empire". The German Question was resolved on October 3, 1990, with the approval of the four former occupying powers, when the German Democratic Republic acceded to the Federal Republic of Germany. At a state act in the Berlin Philharmonie Richard von Weizsäcker, the German President, described the historical importance of **reunification** in a sentence that has gone down in the annals of German history: "The day has come on which for the first time in history the whole of Germany takes a permanent place among Western democracies."

Between 1806 and 1990 there were indeed periods in which Europe was not concerned by what we call "the German Question". Between 1871 and 1914, the peacetime of the Kaiserreich, nobody would have referred to an unresolved German Question. There can be no denying that the German Question resurfaced at the latest on May 8 and 9, 1945 when the German Reich surrendered unconditionally to the victors of the Second World War. The division of Germany into two states was a preliminary answer to the German Question. The final answer came with the merger of the two states and recognition under international law of the borders of 1945. Since October 3, 1990 it has been irrefutably laid down where Germany lies, what belongs to the country and what does not.

Reunification
Following the peaceful overthrow of the East German regime in 1989, reunification of the two Germanies moved that step closer. In the summer of 1990 negotiations about the reunification treaty commenced in Berlin. On October 3, 1990 on the basis of Article 23 of the Basic Law, East Germany acceded to the territory of the Federal Republic of Germany. On December 2, 1990 the first all-German elections to the Bundestag took place.

1830-1848: The Vormärz and Paulskirche parliamentary movement

Holy Roman Empire
The term used for the empire, which emerged from the East-Franconian Empire as of 962, with the coronation of Otto I as Emperor; as of 1512 it was officially called the Holy Roman Empire of the German Nation - expressing, on the one hand, a claim to power as the successor to the "Imperium Romanum" of Antiquity, and on the other, highlighting the religious role of the Emperor. The "Reich" survived for more than eight hundred years until in 1806, shortly after the formation of the Confederation of the Rhine and at the instruction of Napoleon, Franz II, the Habsburg monarch, laid down the imperial crown.

German Confederation
The loose association of sovereign German states and free cities was created at the 1815 Congress of Vienna. It initially comprised 41, and ultimately 33 members. The purpose behind the confederation was primarily the internal and external security of all its members. The Confederation had a single organ: The Federal Assembly in Frankfurt/Main. The conflict with Austria, which had been gaining in strength since the mid-19th century, led to the demise of the German Confederation. It was dissolved in 1866.

For the Germans there were always two sides to the German Question: that of territory and that of constitution, or to be more precise, the question of the relationship between unity and freedom. At the heart of the territorial question was the problem of a "larger Germany" or "smaller Germany". If it were possible to replace the **Holy Roman Empire** with a German national state, would it have to include German-speaking Austria or was a solution to the German Question possible without these territories? The question of the constitution related primarily to the distribution of power between the people and the throne. In a united Germany who was to call the shots: the elected representatives of the Germans or the princes respectively their most powerful choice?

Unity and freedom first emerged as issues in the wars of liberation against Napoleon. The French Emperor was beaten but the removal of the foreign rulers brought the Germans neither a united Germany nor liberal conditions in the states of the **German Confederation** that in 1815 replaced the Old Reich. Yet the call for unity and freedom could no longer be suppressed permanently. In the early 1830s it once again became louder, the French having won their struggle for a liberal constitutional monarchy in the July 1830 revolution. And although in Germany the old rulers were once again able to get their way, from now on the Liberals and Democrats no longer remained silent. Inspired by events in France in February, in March 1848 there was a revolution in Germany, too: Unity and freedom were once again what the forces that knew historical progress was on their side demanded.

To make Germany both a nation and a constitutional state was a far more ambitious goal than that the French revolutionaries had set themselves in 1789, as their starting point was a nation state, which, albeit somewhat pre-modern, already existed and they therefore planned to place it on a completely new, civil basis. Anyone

The "Hambacher Fest", 1832: A highlight of bourgeois opposition to "Vormärz"

demanding unity and freedom for the Germans first of all needed to clarify what was actually to be part of Germany. In the first freely elected parliament, the National Assembly, which convened in the **Paulskirche** in Frankfurt/Main, the fact that a German nation state should include the German-speaking part of the Habsburg monarchy was initially beyond dispute. It was only as of fall 1848 that a majority of the Deputies came to the conclusion that it was not within their power to break up the multi-nation state of Austria-Hungary. Accordingly, as a "large" German state that included Austria could not be established, all that remained possible was a "small" German national state without Austria, and as things stood that meant a Reich under a hereditary Prussian Emperor.

The German state which, according to the will of the National Assembly in Frankfurt/Main, would have been headed by Frederick William IV of Prussia, would have been a liberal constitutional state with a strong parliament that had the government under its control. As German Emperor, the King of Prussia, of the House of the Hohenzollern, would have had to forego the divine right of kings and succumb to being the executor of the superior will of the people. It was a notion that on April 28, 1849 the monarch finally rejected, effectively sealing the fate of the revolution, which had thus brought the Germans neither unity nor freedom. What remained among the bourgeois Liberals was a feeling of political failure: they had, or so it seemed retrospectively, chased down countless illusions in that "mad year" and the realities of power proved them wrong.

It was not by chance that a few years after the 1848 revolution, "Realpolitik" was to become a political catchword: The term's international career began with a pamphlet entitled "The Principles of Realpolitik. Applied to Conditions in the German States", which the Liberal journalist Ludwig August von Rochau brought out in 1853. The Paulskirche had in fact already pursued a policy of "Realpolitik" when it ignored the right of self-determination of other peoples (the Poles in the Prussian Grand Duchy of Posen, the Danes in

Paulskirche 1848
The "March Revolution" that occurred between March 1848 and the summer of 1849 was a national, democratic civil uprising such as was taking place in several parts of Europe at that time. It was a first attempt to create a free, democratic and unified German nation state. The "German Revolution" enforced the appointment of liberal governments and pushed through elections to a National Assembly to draw up a constitution; it was convened in the Paulskirche in Frankfurt/Main. By July 1849 the movement had been violently suppressed by the troops of the German princes and the status quo ante for the most part restored.

Otto von Bismarck (1815–1898)
The unification of Germany under Prussian supremacy was the avowed aim of Otto von Bismarck, whom King Wilhelm I had appointed Prime Minister of Prussia in 1862. Following the 1866 war against Austria, the German Confederation was dissolved and replaced by the North German Confederation, which comprised 17 small German states under Prussian leadership. The victory over France in 1870/1 led to the foundation of the Second German Reich and the proclamation in Versailles of Wilhelm I as German Emperor. Bismarck remained Prime Minister and also became Reich Chancellor. The Reichstag was restructured as the people's elected representation, albeit with restricted rights. Bismarck led a bitter fight against leftwing liberalism, political Catholicism and social democracy, but in the 1880s was also responsible for the most progressive welfare legislation in the whole of Europe. Conflicts with Emperor Wilhelm II, who had been in power since 1888, led in 1890 to the dismissal of the "Iron Chancellor".

North Schleswig, and the Italians in "Welsch Tyrol") and decided to define the borders of the future German Reich in line with supposedly German national interests. As such, unity was for the first time given a higher standing than freedom. The freedom of other nations still had to play second fiddle to the goal of German unity.

1871: Founding of the German Reich

In the 1860s, however, Germany likewise took the decision to prioritize unity over freedom. This was the result of the "revolution from above", by which **Otto von Bismarck**, the Prussian Prime Minister, solved the German Question in his own way. The Prussian constitutional conflict, which lasted from 1862 to 1866, enabled him to solve the question of domestic power in favor of the Executive and against Parliament; in terms of foreign policy a solution to the question of power was delivered by Prussian victory in 1866 in the "smaller Germany" war, i.e., the exclusion of Austria, and in the Franco-Prussian war of 1870/1, against the France of Napoleon III, the power that until then had vetoed the creation of a German nation state.

One goal of the 1848 Revolution had thus been achieved: unity. However, the demand for freedom, inasmuch as it denoted a government responsible to parliament, remained unfulfilled. Even if it had been his intention Bismarck would have been unable to solve the freedom question in the interest of the Liberals: Ceding power to Parliament fundamentally contradicted not only the interests of the ruling classes in old Prussia – of his dynasty, his army, the landed gentry, and high-ranking civil servants. It also contradicted the interests of the other German states, at the top of the list Bavaria, Saxony, and Württemberg. In the form of the Bundesrat they were entitled to a major share of the executive power in the German Reich and were not inclined to forego this power and grant it to the Reichstag. The Reichstag was elected on the basis of universal and equal suffrage by men who had reached

The Iron Chancellor: Otto von Bismarck shaped politics for almost three decades

the age of majority. This was in line with the Reich Constitution of 1849, which never actually came into power and gave the Germans more democratic rights than those enjoyed at the time by the citizens of liberal model monarchies such as Great Britain and Belgium.

As a result one can talk of a partial democratization of Germany in the 19th century, or in relation to the total life span of the German Reich, of dissynchronic democratization: Suffrage was democratized relatively early on, the system of government in the narrow sense, late.

Before the Battle of Verdun, 1916: Over 700,000 German and French soldiers lost their lives

1914–1918: The First World War

It was not until October 1918, when there could no longer be any doubt about Germany's military defeat in the **First World War**, that the decisive change to the constitution occurred, making the Reich Chancellor dependent on the confidence of the Reichstag. This act of making him responsible to Parliament was intended to encourage the victorious Western democracies to condone a lenient peace agreement and preempt a revolution from below. It failed on both counts, but from then on it was easy for the opponents of democracy to denounce the parliamentary system as "Western" and "un-German".

The revolution from below broke out in November 1918 because the October Reforms proved to be nothing more than a piece of paper: Large parts of the military were unwilling to subordinate themselves to political control by Reich leaders that were responsible to Parliament. However, the German Revolution of 1918/9 cannot be considered as one of the major or classic revolutions of world history: Germany around 1918 was already too "modern" for a radical break with its political and social fabric along the lines of the French Revolution of 1789 or the October Revolution of 1917 in Russia. In a country that at a national level had enjoyed universal and general suffrage for men for some 50 years, the issue could not be to establish a revolutionary educational dictatorship but more democracy. In concrete terms

The First World War
When it began the First World War (1914–1918) was fought between the German Empire and Austria, on the one side, and the Triple Entente of France, Great Britain, and Russia together with Serbia, on the other. As it progressed, other countries in Europe, Asia, Africa and America also joined in, including in 1917 the USA, whose entry was to prove decisive. The War resulted in almost 15 million casualties. The military defeat of the German Reich was followed by political upheaval: As a direct consequence of the revolution in November 1918, Emperor Wilhelm II signed a declaration of abdication. The monarchy ceded to a republic.

The Weimar Republic
On November 9, 1918 Philipp Scheidemann, a Social Democrat, proclaimed the republic. It was later named after the city of Weimar, where the National Assembly that drew up the constitution convened. During the Weimar Republic (1919–1933) the German Reich – as the country continued to be called – was a democratic federal state, a mixture of presidential and parliamentary systems. This second attempt to set up a liberal democracy along Western lines in Germany also failed. Ridden by strife, it ended in the National Socialists seizing power, which resulted in a totalitarian dictatorship.

that meant: the introduction of women's suffrage, making suffrage democratic in the individual states, districts and communities and the establishment of governments answerable to parliament.

1919–1933: The Weimar Republic

There was in fact considerable continuity between the German Reich and the **Weimar Republic**, which emerged following the fall of the monarchy in November 1918 and the January 1919 elections to the German National Assembly, which was to draw up a constitution. To a certain extent the institution of the monarchy simply persisted in a different form: The office of Reich President, who was elected by the people, came with such powers that there was very quickly talk of a "substitute Emperor" or a "replacement Emperor".

Nor was there any ethical break with the German Reich. The question of responsibility for the war was not addressed in a serious manner even though (or because) Germany's actions spoke a very clear language: Following the assassination on June 28, 1914 in Sarajevo of the successor to the Austrian-Hungarian throne, the leaders of the Reich deliberately escalated the crisis and therefore bore the main responsibility for the outbreak of the First World War. The subsequent lack of debate about bearing the blame for the war resulted in the German legend that the country was indeed innocent of starting the war. Together with the the "stab-in-the-back-legend" (which claimed that treason on the home front had led to Germany's defeat) this played a part in the undermining of the first German democracy.

Champion of the Labor movement: Rosa Luxemburg was murdered in 1919 during the turmoil of the Revolution in Berlin

Almost all Germans saw the Treaty of Versailles, which Germany was forced to sign on June 28, 1919, as a blatant injustice. This was primarily as a result of the territories the country had to cede, in particular to the newly established Poland, to material hardships in the form of reparation payments, the loss of colonies, and the military restrictions, all

Dance on the Volcano: Otto Dix captured Bohemian life in Berlin ("Großstadt", 1927)

of which were justified by citing the guilt of the German Reich and its allies for the Great War.

The fact that Austria was forbidden to unite with Germany was likewise considered to be unjust. Once the downfall of the Habsburg monarchy had removed the major obstacle to a solution for a greater Germany, the revolutionary governments in Vienna and **Berlin** had spoken out in favor of the two German-speaking republics uniting. They could be assured of the popularity of the demand in both countries.

The fact the Treaties of Versailles and Saint Germain forbade the union did not, however, prevent the notion of a greater Germany once again gaining momentum. It went hand in hand with the renaissance of the old idea of the Reich: Especially because Germany had been beaten militarily and was suffering from the consequences of defeat, it was receptive to the lures that emanated from a past seen through rosy eyes. The Holy Roman Empire in the Middle Ages had not been a nation state but rather a supranational structure with universal claims. After 1918, forces on the political right, who attributed a new mission to Germany, made increasing reference to this legacy: In Europe, they suggested, it should establish itself as the upholder of law and order in the struggle against Western democracy and Eastern Bolshevism.

As a parliamentary democracy the Weimar Republic survived a mere 11 years. At the end of March 1930, the

Berlin in the "Golden Twenties "
Between 1924 and 1929, the period of economic upswing and political calm led to a brief but highly productive period, whose presence was felt most of all in the capital city Berlin. The metropolis became one of Europe's cultural and scientific hot spots. Technological advances and artistic experimentation in architecture, theater, literature and film all enhanced the overall joie de vivre. The world economic crisis of 1929 was a harbinger of the end of the "Golden Twenties" and the decline of the Weimar Republic.

German history

From the early Middle Ages via the Reformation and the catastrophes of the 20th century through to reunification: Stages in German history

962
Otto I or Otto the Great
His crowning as emperor marks the start of the "Holy Roman Empire"

1024–1125/1138–1268
Salier and Staufer
The dynasties of the Salier (builders of **Speyer Cathedral**, photo) and Staufer families shape the destiny of Europe

1452–1454
Invention of printing
Johannes Gutenberg (c. 1400–1468), inventor of printing with movable type, produces the first printed Bible in Mainz – roughly 180 copies

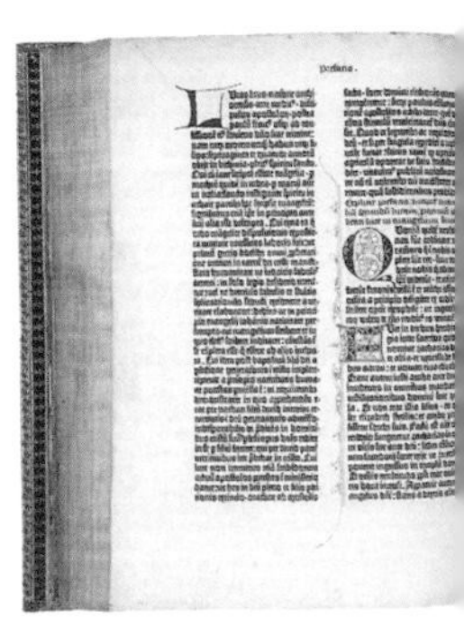

800 | 900 | 1000 | 1100 | 1200 | 1300

8th century | 9th century | 10th century | 11th century | 12th century | 13th century | 14

800
Charlemagne
The ruler of the Frankish Empire is crowned Roman emperor by Pope Leo III. Later the Carolingian, who dies 814 in Aachen, is declared the "Father of Europe"

1179
Hildegard von Bingen
The abbess and healer, one of the most influential women in medieval Germany, dies aged 81 in Bingen on Rhine

1493
Rise of the House of Habsburg
The regency of **Maximilian I** marks the rise of the House of Habsburg. For centuries it was one of the dominant aristocratic dynasties in Central Europe, supplied the majority of emperors and kings of the Holy Roman Empire of the German Nation, and from 1504-1700 the kings of Spain

1803
Secularization
The secularization of ecclesiastical rule and the dissolution of Imperial free cities by the Final Recess (Reichsdeputationshauptschluss) herald the end of the "Holy Roman Empire of the German Nation"

1618-1648
Thirty Years' War
Both a religious war and political conflict, the Thirty Years' War ends with the Peace of Westphalia: The Catholic, Lutheran and Reformist faiths are recognized as equal

1740-1786
Frederick the Great
During the reign of Frederick II, literary scholar and general, Prussia emerges as a European superpower. His rule is seen as exemplary for the age of "enlightened absolutism"

1848/49
March Revolution
The "German Revolution" begins in the Grand Duchy of Baden. Before long it spreads to the other states of the German Federation and leads to the first German National Assembly, which convened in the **Paulskirche**, Frankfurt/Main

1400 | 1500 | 1600 | 1700 | 1800 | 1900

...ury | 15th century | 16th century | 17th century | 18th century | 19th century | 20th century

1517
Religious schism
The Age of the Reformation begins when **Martin Luther** (1483-1546) publicly declares his 95 Theses against the system of indulgences in the Catholic Church in Wittenberg

1871
Foundation of the Reich
On January 18 during the Franco-Prussian War **Wilhelm I** is proclaimed German Emperor in Versailles. The (second) German Reich is a constitutional monarchy. Shortly before the foundation of the empire the nation experienced an economic upswing known as the "Gründerjahre"

German history

1914–1918
World War I
Emperor **Wilhelm II** isolates Germany from its neighbors and leads the country into the catastrophe of the First World War, which costs the lives of almost 15 million people. In June 1919 the Treaty of Versailles is signed, ending the war

1918/19
Weimar Republic
On November 9, 1918 Social Democrat **Philipp Scheidemann** proclaims the Republic; Emperor Wilhelm II abdicates. On January 19, 1919 elections are held for the National Assembly

1933
National Socialism
The NSDAP gains the most votes in the Reichstag elections in 1932; on January 30 1933 **Adolf Hitler** becomes Chancellor of the Reich. The National Socialist dictatorship begins with the "Enabling Act"

1939
Start of the Second World War
Through his invasion of Poland on September 1, 1939 Hitler unleashes the Second World War, which cost 60 million people their lives and devastated large parts of Europe and East Asia. The Nazi extermination policy results in the murder of six million Jews

1945
The Second World War ends
The capitulation of the German Wehrmacht between May 7-9, 1945 ends the Second World War in Europe. The four Allies divide the country into four occupation zones and Berlin into four sectors

1948
Blockade of Berlin
The introduction of the deutschmark in the Western occupation zones prompts the Soviet Union on June 14, 1948 to cut off access to West-Berlin. The Allies respond with an airlift dropping supplies to the population in West Berlin until September 1949

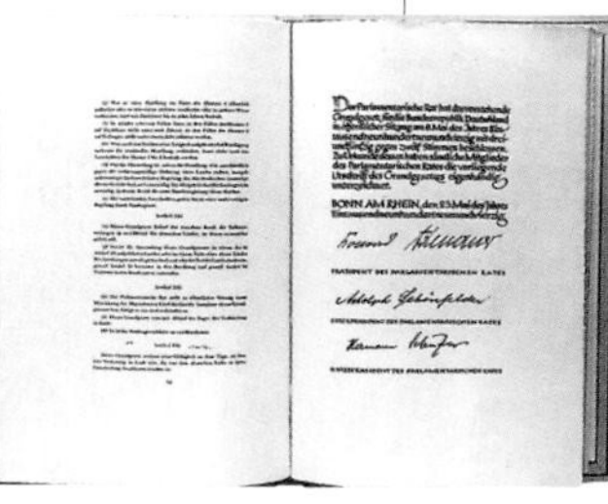

1949
Birth of the Federal Republic of Germany
On May 23, 1949 the Basic Law of the Federal Republic of Germany is proclaimed in Bonn. The first parliamentary elections are held on August 14. **Konrad Adenauer** (CDU) is elected Chancellor. On October 7, 1949 the division between East and West is completed when the Constitution of the German Democratic Republic comes into force

1957
Treaties of Rome
The Federal Republic of Germany is one of the six nations to sign the founding treaties of the European Economic Community

1910 1920 1930 1940 1950

20th century

1963
Elysée Treaty
The Treaty of Friendship between France and Germany is signed by West German Chancellor **Konrad Adenauer** (right) and the French President **Charles de Gaulle**

1970
Brandt kneels in Warsaw
The gesture by West German Chancellor **Willy Brandt** (SPD) before the memorial for the victims of the uprising in the Jewish ghetto in Warsaw became a symbol of the German plea for reconciliation

1990
German reunification
On October 3, East Germany formally ceases to exist. Germany's political unity is restored. The first general elections of the united Germany are held on December 2, 1990. **Helmut Kohl** (CDU) becomes the unified nation's first Chancellor

1970 1980 1990 2000 2010

21st century

1961
Building of the Berlin Wall
East Germany cuts itself off on August 13, 1961 by erecting a wall through the middle of Berlin and the "Death Strip" along the border between the two Germanies

1989
The Fall of the Wall
The peaceful revolution in East Germany leads in November 9 to the Berlin Wall coming down and with it the border between East and West Germany

2004/2007
EU Expansion
Following the disintegration of the Soviet Union and the fall of Communism, in 2004 eight Central and East European nations plus Cyprus and Malta joined the EU, followed in 2007 by Bulgaria and Romania

National Socialism
National Socialism was the result of a broad-based anti-Semitic, nationalist movement that from 1920 on found expression in the National Socialist German Workers' Party (NSDAP). The main features of the National Socialist ideology were racism, in particular, anti-Semitism, and the propagation of an Aryan master race, social Darwinism that justified euthanasia and eugenics, totalitarianism and the rejection of democracy, the "alignment of the people" in the sense of their adopting the principle of a Fuehrer, militarism, chauvinism and the ideology of a biologically founded "community of people", imperialism disguised as "Lebensraum" policy as well as the propaganda events to whip up grass roots support.

last majority government, headed by Hermann Müller, a Social Democrat, collapsed on the back of an argument about restructuring the unemployment insurance system. The Grand Coalition that had been in power until then was replaced by a center-right minority cabinet under a politician from the Catholic Zentrum Party, Heinrich Brüning. From the summer of 1930, this government ruled with the help of emergency decrees issued by General Field Marshall Paul von Hindenburg, the aging Reich President.

When at the Reichstag elections held on September 14, 1930 Adolf Hitler's Nationalist Socialist Party (NSDAP) became the second biggest party, the Social Democrat Party (SPD), which was still the largest party, decided to tolerate the Brüning cabinet in order to prevent the Reich drifting further to the right and to preserve democracy in Prussia, the largest individual state, where the SPD ruled jointly with Brüning's Catholic Center Party, and the center-right Democrats.

Following the transition to a presidential system of emergency decree, as a legislative body the Reichstag had less influence than during the constitutional monarchy of the German Reich. The decreased influence of parliament meant that to a large extent the electorate no longer played any role in the running of the country, and it was precisely this that gave a boost to anti-parliamentarian forces on the right and left. Of these the National Socialists benefited the most. From the point in time when the Social Democrats supported Brüning, Hitler was able to present his party as the people's only alternative to all forms of Marxism, the Bolshevist just as much as the Reformist. He was now in a position to refer to both: to the widespread resentment of parliamentary democracy (which indeed had by now well and truly failed) and to the people's secured claim to participation in the shape of universal and equal suffrage, which they had enjoyed since the days of Bismarck and which had been rendered politically ineffective by the three presidential governments of Brüning, Papen and Schleicher in the early 1930s.

A culture of remembrance: Bundeswehr soldiers remember the victims of Hitler's dictatorship

Thus, Hitler became the greatest beneficiary of the dissynchronic democratization of Germany, namely the introduction of democratic suffrage well before that of a parliamentary system of government.

1933–1945: The era of National Socialism

Hitler did not come to power on the back of a major election victory but he would not have become Reich Chancellor in January 1933 had he not been the leader of the strongest party. At the last Weimar Republic Reichstag elections on November 6, 1932 the National Socialists had lost two million votes compared with the July 31, 1932 elections, while the Communists gained 600,000 thereby reaching the magic number of 100 Reichstag seats. The success of the Communist Party (KPD) whipped up fears of civil war, and it was this fear that was to become Hitler's most powerful ally, particularly among the powerful Conservative elite. It was their recommendation to Hindenburg that Hitler had to thank for the fact that on January 30, 1933 the Reich President appointed him to the position of Reich Chancellor at the head of a predominantly conservative cabinet.

Terror against anyone who dissented was not a sufficient means to hold on to power during the 12 years of the Third Reich. Hitler was able to beat unemployment within a matter of years primarily through a rearmaments program, thereby winning the support of large sections of the working classes. As a result of the ruthless exploitation of workers and natural resources in the occupied territories he had been able to spare the German masses the hardships they had had to endure after the First World War, ensuring that he could count on their support even during the Second World War. The major successes in foreign policy during the pre-War years, headed by the reoccupation of the de-militarized Rhineland in March 1936 and the Austrian "Anschluss" in March 1938 meant that Hitler's popularity was to reach record levels in all classes

The Third Reich
The twelve years of National Socialist rule between 1933 and 1945 are referred as the so-called "Third Reich". It began with the appointment of Hitler as Reich Chancellor on January 30, 1933 and ended with the unconditional capitulation of the German Wehrmacht on May 7, 1945. The "Third Reich" is a synonym for the unrestrained propaganda of racist and anti-Semitic ideology, with political and social organizations being robbed of any independence from the state, the ideological permeation of public life, the terror against the Jews and dissidents; it can likewise be equated with euphoric mass support and industrialized mass murder, an uncontrolled lust for expansion as well as the instigation of the Second World War.

60 years after the end of war: Gerhard Schroeder (left) is the first German Chancellor to attend celebrations to mark the end of the Second World War in Moscow

Central memorial site: In May 2005 the memorial for the murdered Jews of Europe is opened in Berlin

The Holocaust
The Holocaust refers to the systematic, bureaucratically planned and the industrially perfected murder of six million European Jews. Sinti and Roma, homosexuals and other people that the Nazis deemed "unwanted" or "not worthy of living" were also victims. In an unimaginable extermination program these persons were exploited, tortured, humiliated and murdered in death factories and concentration camps. The deaths were preceded by the propaganda-driven enforcement of a racist, anti-Semitic ideology, the swift repeal of civil rights of the Jews, the appropriation of their belongings and their confinement to ghettoes. Not only all state organs but also the military elite, industry, banks, academia and the medical professions were directly involved in the Holocaust.

of society. The legend of the Reich and its historic mission, which Hitler was a master in propagating, influenced in particular educated Germans. The charismatic "Fuehrer" needed their assistance if he was to make Germany a long-term power in the European order, and they needed him, too, because otherwise it seemed there was nobody in a position to make the dream of a great German Reich become reality.

Even though he did not focus on it, in the electoral campaigns in the early 1930s Hitler had made no secret of his anti-Semitism. His slogans would not have won him many votes among the working classes, something he was extremely keen to do. Among educated, property-owning classes, small businessmen and farmers anti-Jewish prejudice was widespread, whereas strident anti-Semitism was frowned upon.

Because they remained within the letter of the law, the Nuremberg Race Laws of September 1935, which deprived Jews of their civil rights, met with no opposition. The violent disturbances during the Reichskristallnacht on November 9, 1938 were unpopular, the "Aryanization" of Jewish property, an enormous re-distribution of assets, the repercussions of which are still being felt today, on the other hand, not. More was actually known about the Holocaust, the systematic extermination of European Jews during the

Second World War, than suited the regime. But knowledge of something also involves a wish to know, something of which, as far as the fate of the Jews was concerned, there was a distinct lack in Germany during the Third Reich.

In German history the downfall of Hitler's Greater German Reich in May 1945 signifies a far deeper caesura than that of the German Reich in November 1918. The Reich as such continued to exist after the First World War. Following the unconditional surrender at the end of the Second World War governmental power and the decision-making powers as to the future of Germany were assumed by the four occupying powers, the United States, the Soviet Union, Great Britain and France. Unlike 1918, in 1945 the German political and military leaders were stripped of their powers and, inasmuch as they were still alive, sent for trial before the International Military Tribunal in Nuremberg. The landowners east of the River Elbe, who had contributed more than any other powerful elite to the destruction of the Weimar Republic and the transfer of power to Hitler lost everything: on the one hand, as a result of the cession of territories to the east of the Oder and Neisse Rivers to Poland, or, in the case of Northeastern Prussia, Soviet administration, and, on the other, due to the "land reform" in the zone under Soviet occupation.

As opposed to the aftermath of 1918, after 1945 the legends of back-stabbing or a lack of guilt for the war fell on as good as deaf ears. It was just too clear-cut that Nazi Germany had unleashed the Second World War and had only been suppressed from without, through the superior might of the Allies. In both the First and Second World Wars German propaganda had portrayed the democratic Western powers as imperialist plutocrats, but their own law and order as an expression of a high level of social justice. After 1945 renewed attacks on the Western democracies would have been crazy: The price paid for the contempt shown for the West's political ideas was too high for a return to the slogans of the past to promise any success.

The Second World War

On September 1, 1939 at 4.45 a.m. Hitler invaded neighboring Poland without having declared war. As a consequence, Great Britain and France declared war on Germany. The Second World War had begun and would result in the loss of 60 million lives. The Soviet Union was to mourn most of the dead – some 25 million. The Germans' Blitzkrieg strategy came to a halt before the gates of Moscow, and the entry into the war of the USA put an end to the unrelenting expansion policy of Germany and her allies. On May 7, 1945 at the Allied Headquarters in Reims in France, Hitler's successor, Karl Dönitz, had General Alfred Jodl, the Commander-in-Chief of the Wehrmacht, sign the unconditional German capitulation.

Nuremberg Trials: The proceedings against war criminals began in November 1945

Basic Law
The Basic Law is the legal and political foundation of the Federal Republic of Germany. It was originally thought of as a temporary solution and provisional arrangement until such time as a constitution for the whole of Germany could be drawn up. When the GDR acceded to the area of validity of the Basic Law on October 3, 1990 it became the constitution of the whole of Germany. The Basic Law stands for the success story of democracy in Germany following Nazi rule and is seen as a stroke of luck for German history.

East Germany
The German Democratic Republic (GDR), as East Germany was officially called, was founded in 1949 in the Soviet occupation zone and the East sector of Berlin and existed until October 2, 1990. It formed part of the Eastern bloc, which was under the hegemony of the Soviet Union. During the 1953 uprising there were nationwide demonstrations, which, aided by the East German police (Volkspolizei), were put down by the Soviet military.

June 17, 1953: People in over 400 towns demonstrate against the East German leadership

1949–1990: The two German states

After 1945 only one part of Germany had a chance to give democracy a second go, namely West Germany. In 1948/9, representatives of the freely elected parliaments of the federal states in the American, British and French zones of occupation met in the Parliamentary Council in Bonn and devised a constitution that drew logical conclusions from the mistakes made in preparing the Reich Constitution of 1919 and the failure of the Weimar Republic: The Basic Law of the Federal Republic of Germany. This second German democracy was to be a functioning parliamentary democracy with a strong Federal Chancellor, who could only be toppled by a "constructive vote of no confidence", i.e., by a successor being voted, and a Federal President who played a nominal role only. As opposed to Weimar days, parallel legislative powers for the people were not envisaged. The Basic Law put a shot across the bows of any self-confessed opponents of democracy, by stating that the fight for basic rights and a ban on political parties that were not in line with the constitution would be taken as far as the Federal Constitutional Court. The principles of the state were given very strong foundations by making it impossible even for a majority vote to change the constitution, rendering the "legal" elimination of democracy, as in 1933, impossible.

While the West of Germany drew "anti-totalitarian" conclusions from the most recent German history, the East, that is the Soviet zone of occupation and later East Germany, had to put up with "anti-fascist" consequences. These served to legitimize a Marxist-Leninist-influenced party dictatorship. The break with the principles of Nazi rule was to be achieved primarily through class struggle, by dispossessing large landowners and industrialists. Former Nazi "supporters", by contrast, were to be allowed to prove their worth to society by helping "build socialism". Once the process of "denazification" had been completed, in East Germany former Nazi party officials also managed to occupy leading positions. They were, however, fewer and their cases less spectacular than in West Germany.

In retrospect, had it not been for the "economic miracle" in the 1950s and 1960s, the longest boom period in the 20th century, there could hardly have been talk of a success story with regard to West Germany. The booming economy gave legitimacy to the model of a social market economy promulgated by Ludwig Erhard, the first Federal Economics Minister by virtue of its success. It enabled the swift integration of the eight million displaced persons from the former Eastern territories of the German Reich, the Sudetenland and other areas of East and Southeast Europe.

It made a decisive contribution to class and religious differences being eliminated, to the attraction of radical parties being curbed, and to the major democratic parties, initially the Christian Democrat (CDU) and the Christian Social Union (CSU), followed by the Social Democratic Party (SPD) becoming major popular parties. With regard to politics and social mores, however, there was also a different side to this prosperity: It made it easier for many citizens of West Germany neither to ask themselves searching questions about their own role in the years between 1933 and 1945, nor to let others ask them about it. The philosopher Hermann Lübbe referred to this approach to recent history as "communicative refusing to mention" (and judged it to be necessary in the stabilizing of West German democracy).

In the Weimar Republic the right had been nationalist and the left internationalist. In West Germany it was a different story: the center right camp under the first Federal Chancellor Konrad Adenauer stood for a policy of alignment with the West and the supranational integration of western Europe; the moderate left, the Social Democrats under their first post-War Chairman Kurt Schumacher and his successor Erich Ollenhauer, gave themselves a decidedly national profile by favoring reunification ahead of integration in the West. It was not until 1960 that the SPD accepted the basis of the West Treaties, which in 1955 had enabled West Germany to join NATO.

Symbol on wheels: The VW-Beetle stands for German economic recovery in the 1950s

Economic miracle

The term "economic miracle" refers to West Germany's swift economic recovery following the Second World War. The prerequisites were the reconstruction of production facilities to the highest technical standards, the introduction of the deutschmark and massive financial support on the part of the USA through the Marshall Plan. By the late 1950s Germany had emerged as one of the leading economic nations.

Konrad Adenauer (1876–1967)

The Christian Democrat was the first Chancellor of the Federal Republic of Germany. He was head of government from 1949 until 1963. As a result of his unflinching West-oriented policies he integrated Germany into the international community, NATO and the European Economic Community (EEC). His achievements also include reconciliation with France and his attempts at reconciliation with Israel.

Willy Brandt (1913–1992)
The Social Democrat was Chancellor of the Federal Republic from 1969 until 1974. In 1971, Brandt was awarded the Nobel Peace prize for his policy of Ostpolitik, which aimed to promote entente and political balance with East European states (the "policy of small steps"). His policy of detente contributed to the emergence of the Organization for Security and Cooperation in Europe (OSCE).

The Social Democrats had to make this step if they were to assume governmental responsibility in West Germany. Only on the basis of the West Treaties were they able, in 1966, to become a junior partner in the Grand Coalition and three years later, under the first Social Democrat Federal Chancellor Willy Brandt, begin the "new Ostpolitik" that enabled West Germany to make a contribution to easing tension between West and East, to put relations with Poland on a new footing by the recognition (even if not completely unconditionally de jure) of the Oder-Neisse line and to enter into a contractually regulated relationship with East Germany.

The 1971 Four Powers Agreement on Berlin, which actually only concerned West Berlin and its relations with West Germany, would also have been impossible without the larger of the two Germanies being firmly integrated in the West.

The series of treaties with Eastern Europe signed by the liberal Brandt-Scheel government between 1970 and 1973 was primarily one thing: a response to the harder shape taken by the division of Germany with the building of the Berlin Wall on August 13, 1961. With reunification becoming an ever more distant prospect, West Germany was forced into making the consequences of this division more sufferable, thereby ensuring the cohesion of the nation. The re-establishment of German unity remained an official goal of West German policy. However, following signature of the treaties with the East, the expectation that there would ever again be a German nation state dwindled – much more among younger Germans than among the more elderly.

Winner of the Nobel Peace Prize 1971: Willy Brandt

In the 1980s, though, the post-War fabric gradually began to tear. The crisis in the Eastern bloc began in 1980, with the founding of an independent trade union, "Solidarnosc" , in Poland, followed by the imposition of martial law at the end of 1981. Three-and-a-half years later, in March 1985, Michael Gorbachev came to power in the Soviet Union.

International politics in the Caucasus: German Chancellor Kohl, Kremlin leader Gorbachev and German Foreign Minister Genscher (from r to l) clarified unsettled issues relating to reunification in summer 1990

In January 1987 the new Secretary General of the Communist Party of the Soviet Union uttered the almost revolutionary statement: "We need democracy like the air we breathe." A message like this was an added boost to civil rights activists in Poland and Hungary, in Czechoslovakia and in East Germany. In fall 1989 the pressure from the protests in East Germany became so great that the communist regime could only have been saved by military intervention on the part of the Soviet Union. Gorbachev, however, was not prepared to do this. This ultimately caused the party leadership in East Berlin to capitulate to the peaceful revolution in East Germany: On November 9, 1989 the Berlin Wall fell – a symbol of the restriction of freedom similar to the Bastille in Paris two hundred years before.

Peaceful Revolution
Within just a few weeks in the autumn of 1989, the East German population staged a spontaneous, non-violent revolution to bring down the ruling authorities. On November 9, 1989 the Berlin Wall, the very symbol of the division of Germany and the Cold War, fell. The event was preceded by the mass exodus of East German citizens, who fled the country via Prague, Warsaw and the now open border between Hungary and Austria, as well as huge demonstrations, in particular in Leipzig, public protests by famous personalities and civil rights protestors and the increasing demand for freedom to travel.

1990: Reunification

With the Wall having fallen in 1989, it was to be another 11 months before Germany was reunited. Germans in both German states welcomed it. In the first (and last) free elections to East Germany's Volkskammer (parliament) on March 18, 1990 the East German electorate voted by an overwhelming majority for those parties that demanded swift accession to West Germany.

In summer 1990 a treaty to this effect was negotiated by the two Germanies, as had the treaty concerning the German-German currency union. Parallel to this in

The Two-plus-Four-Treaty
This refers to the "final provisions with respect to Germany" of September 12, 1990, which was signed in Moscow by the two Germanies and the four victors of the Second World War (France, Great Britain, the Soviet Union and the USA) to safeguard German unity with regard to foreign policy. The treaty re-established the full sovereign unity of Germany. It proclaimed Germany's borders as final and that the country had no claim to former German territories.

the Two-plus-Four-Treaty West and East Germany reached agreement with the four powers responsible for Berlin and Germany as a whole, i.e., the United States, the Soviet Union, Great Britain and France on the conditions with regard to foreign and security policy determining German unity.

In terms of the old demand for "unity in freedom" the German Question was finally solved in 1990. It could only be solved with the approval of all the country's neighbors, which also meant: with the solution at the same time of another problem that had dominated the century: the Polish Question. The final recognition, binding under international law, of the fact that the Oder and Neisse Rivers formed the western border of Poland was a precondition of the reunification of Germany in the borders of 1945.

Post-reunification Germany sees itself not as a "postnational democracy among nation states", as the political scientist Karl Dietrich Bracher once termed the "old" Federal Republic in 1976, but rather a post-classical democratic national state among others – firmly embedded in the Atlantic Alliance and in the supranational confederation of states that is the European Union (EU), in which certain aspects of national sovereignty are pursued jointly with other member states. There is much here that distinguishes the second German state from the first – namely everything that had made Bismarck's Reich a military and authoritarian state.

Large collection: The Deutsche Historische Museum, Berlin, owns some 700,000 objects on German history

The topic on the Internet

www.dhm.de
The Deutsche Historische Museum in Berlin provides an insight into Germany's history (English, German). The "Lebendige Museum Online" www.dhm.de/lemo (German) is also of interest

www.hdg.de
Das Haus der Geschichte der Bundesrepublik Deutschland provides information about modern history, also by means of virtual exhibitions (English, German, French)

www.wege-der-erinnerung.de
A joint European Web project to do with the wars and conflicts in the first half of the 20th century (English, German, French, Italian, Dutch, Spanish)

www.holocaust-mahnmal.de
The Web memorial to the murdered European Jews (English, German)

www.historikerverband.de
The Web site of the Verband der Historiker und Historikerinnen Deutschlands, Europe's largest association of historians (German)

There is, however, also some form of continuity between the first and the second nation state. As a democratic constitutional state, a federal and welfare state the reunited Federal Republic of Germany very much follows traditions that date well back to the 19th century. The same applies to the universal, equal suffrage and the parliamentary culture, which had emerged in the Reichstag during the German Reich. A certain geographical continuity is also clearly evident: The Two-plus-Four-Treaty, the constitutional founding document of the reunited Federal Republic of Germany, once again outlined in writing the smaller German solution, the existence of the separate states of Germany and Austria.

The German Question has been resolved since 1990, but the European Question remains open. Since the expansions to the EU in 2004 and 2007, the EU has included 12 additional nations, of which ten were under Communist rule until the dawn of the new epoch between 1989 and 1991. They are all states that belong to the former Occident – and which have been defined by a largely shared legal tradition, the early separation of religious and state powers, princely and civil powers, not to forget by the experience of the murderous consequences of religious and national enmity, and racial hatred. It will take time for those parts of Europe that were once divided to grow closer together. This will only succeed if European unity develops at the same pace as the Union has expanded. This development requires more than institutional reforms. It hinges on joint deliberation on European history and its consequences. The one consequence that is more important than all others is an appreciation of the overall binding nature of Western values, first and foremost inalienable human rights. These are the values that Europe and America have created together, which they uphold, and by which they must at all times be measured. •

Heinrich August Winkler
One of the leading German historians, Prof. Winkler was Professor at the Humboldt University in Berlin until retiring in 2007. His work "Der lange Weg nach Westen" (Long Road to West) brought him international acclaim.

4

Political system

It fast became a successful model and a prime export: After the Second World War, the Basic Law provided freedom and stability - albeit initially only for the Germans in the West of the nation that remained divided until 1990.

The primacy of the basic rights, the definition of the principles of a democratic and social federal state, and the foundation of a supreme court that watches over adherence to the constitution - these are the basic cornerstones of German democracy.

Symbol of open insight: The dome over the Reichstag building

The state, the legal system and the citizens

By Jürgen Hartmann

THE POLITICAL SYSTEM OF THE FEDERAL REPUBLIC of Germany represents the second democratic system in German history. At the **Parliamentary Council** when designing the new constitution, the Basic Law, the founders of the Federal Republic took into account the lessons that had been learned from the failure of the first democracy, namely the Weimar Republic, and the Nazi dictatorship. The Federal Republic of Germany was born from the ashes of World War II. And in 1949 democracy was initially established only in the Western section of a Germany that had been divided into two states. Yet the Basic Law, although originally intended as a temporary solution, stated that its goal was reunification "in free self-determination".

The second German democracy turned out to be a success. There were several reasons for this, among which were the value placed on a way of life based on the principle of liberty following the dictatorship and a striving for acceptance by the country's democratic neighbors. But the Basic Law also had its role to play in the success. In 1990, when 40 years of German division came to an end, the Basic Law was adopted as the constitution of a united Germany.

Parliamentary Council
The constitutional convention met for the first time on Sept. 1, 1948. It was made up of 65 delegates elected by the West German State Parliaments. Prior to this, an expert working party had met on the island of Herrenchiemsee in Bavaria and compiled the documents for discussion at the convention.

Basic Law
After it had been approved by the Parliamentary Council, the Basic Law came into force on May 23, 1949. It sets out the fundamental legal and political order for the Federal Republic of Germany. The basic rights enshrined in the Basic Law are of particular importance.

The Basic Law

The **Basic Law** ties the legislative process to the constitutional order and binds state administration to uphold the law. Section 1 of the Basic Law is of particular relevance. It stipulates that respect for human dignity is the most important aspect of the constitution: "Human dignity shall be invio-

The Federal coat-of-arms: Black eagle, with red edges on a golden yellow background

lable. To respect and protect it shall be the duty of all state authority." Among other things, the other basic rights guarantee the freedom to act within the law, equality before the law, freedom of the press and media, freedom of association and protection of the family.

In determining that it is the people who exercise power through special bodies, the Basic Law lays down representative democracy as the form of rulership. Furthermore, it determines that Germany is a constitutional state: All state authorities are subject to judicial control. Another principle of the constitution is that Germany is a **federal state**, in other words the ruling authorities are divided up into a number of member states and the central state. In conclusion, the Basic Law defines Germany as a welfare state. The **welfare state** requires the political system to take precautions such that people are guaranteed a decent standard of material well-being in case of unemployment, disability, illness and in old age. One particular feature of the Basic Law is the so-called "eternal character" of these governing constitutional principles. Subsequent alterations to the Basic Law or a completely new constitution cannot encroach on the basic rights, the democratization of sovereignty, the federal state and the welfare state.

Federal state
The Federal Republic of Germany consists of 16 federal states. The powers of the state are divided up between government as a whole, the Federal Government and the federal states. The latter have independent, if limited government authority.

Welfare state
There is a long tradition of the welfare state in Germany. In 1883, the Bill on Health Insurance was enacted, followed in 1884 by that on accident insurance and in 1889 on invalidity and old-age insurance. At that time, only one tenth of the population was protected by this insurance coverage, whereas the figure today is some 90 percent.

Parties in the Bundestag

SPD
Social Democratic Party of Germany
Chairman: **Kurt Beck**
Founded: 1863/1875
Membership: 550,000

CDU
Christian Democratic Union
Chairperson: **Angela Merkel**
Founded: 1945
1950 at the Federal level
Membership: 544,000

CSU
Christian Social Union
Chairman: **Erwin Huber**
Founded: 1945
Membership: 168,000

FDP
Free Democratic Party
Chairman: **Guido Westerwelle**
Founded: 1948
Membership: 65,000

The political parties

According to the Basic Law it is the task of the political parties to participate in political will formation by the people. As such, putting forward candidates for political office and the organization of election campaigns both have the status of constitutional tasks. For this reason the parties are reimbursed the costs they incur in their respective election campaign. The **reimbursement of election campaign costs**, a feature Germany was the first country to introduce, is now commonplace in most democracies. According to the Basic Law, a political party's internal organization must conform to democratic principles (member democracy). And all parties are expected to acknowledge the values and structure of the democratic state.

Parties whose commitment to democracy is in doubt can, at the request of the Federal Government, be banned from participation in the country's political life. However, such a ban is not automatically forthcoming in any sense. Should the Federal Government consider a ban to be appropriate because such parties pose a threat to the democratic system, it can only petition for such a ban. Any such ban may only be enacted by the Federal Constitutional Court after duly considering the individual case. The

Reimbursement of election campaign costs
This is part of the financing received by the political parties, which is made up of contributions by party members, income from assets the party holds, donations and state subsidies. The parties each receive a lump sum from the state toward their election campaign costs; its size depends on the number of votes they last polled and the size of their contributions and donations.

The Greens
Alliance 90/The Greens
Chairpersons: **Claudia Roth, Reinhard Bütikofer**
Founded: 1980
Membership: 45,000

The Left Party
Chairmen: **Lothar Bisky, Oskar Lafontaine**
Founded: 1989
Membership: 69,000

Parties represented in the Bundestag: **SPD** and **CDU/CSU** as well as the **FDP** have been represented in the Bundestag since it was founded. CDU and CSU have a joint parliamentary party. The CSU stands for election in Bavaria, the CDU in all the other federal states. In 1984, the Greens were elected to the Bundestag for the first time; after German unification they joined forces with the East German **Alliance 90**. In 1990, the successor party to the East German Socialist Unity Party, the SED, was elected to the Bundestag under the new name of Party of Democratic Socialism (PDS). In 2005, the PDS renamed itself The Left Party.PDS. In 2007, it merged with WASG, the Electoral Alternative Labor and Social Justice, to form **The Left Party**.

Elections
Every four years, the parties stand in the general elections to the Bundestag. Traditionally, the turn-out is high in Germany, and following a high in the 1970s, when the turn-out was over 90 percent, since reunification it has been around 80 percent. The elections to the 16th German Bundestag on Sept. 18, 2005 saw a turn-out of 77.7 percent of the electorate.

idea is to prevent the ruling parties simply banning those parties who might prove awkward in the fight for votes. The parties in government prefer to combat undemocratic parties in the everyday political arena through political debate on the issues at hand. In the history of the Federal Republic there have been few banning processes, and even fewer parties have actually been banned. Though the Basic Law accords political parties some privileges, these are, basically, means for society to express itself. They take full responsibility for failing at **elections**, a loss of members, or strife in conjunction with personnel and factual issues.

The German party system is quite transparent. Until 1983, the Bundestag was composed only of those parties who had sat in parliament since the very first elections when the Bundestag was first convened back in 1949. They are: the Christian Democratic Union/Christian Social Union (CDU/CSU), the Social Democratic Party of Germany (SPD) and the Free Democratic Party (FDP). With the exception of

The Federal Government

On November 22, 2005 the German Bundestag elected Dr. Angela Merkel (CDU) to the office of Chancellor of the Federal Republic of Germany. She is the leader of a grand coalition of CDU/CSU and SPD. Angela Merkel is the first woman to head a Federal Government. The government consists of five female and ten male ministers. As a joint parliamentary party, the CDU and CSU

provide six ministers as well as the head of the Federal Chancellery Office. The SPD is responsible for eight ministries, including the Federal Foreign Office, headed by the Federal Minister of Foreign Affairs and Vice-Chancellor, Dr. Frank-Walter Steinmeier (SPD).

At the half-way mark in the legislative period, the cabinet felt it had achieved much: Steady growth in GDP and rising employment confirm the validity of its economic and reform policies implemented to date. During its Presidency of the EU Council and as G8 President, Germany influenced foreign and security policies in important areas. It is the Federal Government's express goal to reinforce the economic upturn and the favorable labor market trend. Moreover, it intends to press ahead with its ambitious climate and energy policies.

www.bundesregierung.de

Bavaria, throughout Germany the Union parties, and they are both members of the European Christian Democrat group of parties, stand as the Christian Democratic Union. The CDU itself declines to stand in Bavaria, preferring to leave the region to the Christian Social Union, with which it is closely allied. In the Bundestag the members of parliament of both parties have joined forces to create a permanent **parliamentary party**.

The Social Democratic Party of Germany is the other major force in the German party system. It belongs to the European group of Social Democratic and democratic socialist parties. CDU/CSU and SPD are considered to be the "popular" parties, i. e., in the past they successfully managed to secure the support of a broad cross-section of the **electorate**. In principle, both parties support a welfare state with its guaranteed income for the elderly, sick, disabled and unemployed. Whereas the CDU/CSU attract the self-employed, businessmen and entrepreneurs, the SPD has close links to the unions.

The Free Democratic Party belongs to the European group of liberal parties. Its political creed is that of the state being involved as little as possible in the economy. The FDP is not one of the "popular" parties. It receives backing primarily from well-educated high-earners.

The Alliance 90/The Greens, referred to in short as "The Greens", was founded in 1980 and was the first party founded post-1949 to enjoy long-term success. The Greens belong to the European group of green and ecological parties. The characteristic feature of their program is the combination of market economy and decrees pertaining to nature and environment protection that must be monitored by the state. They too represent higher-income voters with an above-average standard of education.

Following reunification the Party of Democratic Socialism (PDS) entered the political arena in the Federal Republic of Germany. It emerged in 1989 as the successor to the SED, the state socialist party of the former German Democratic Republic. The PDS has transformed itself into a

Parliamentary party
At least five percent of the members of the Bundestag, and they must belong to one and the same party or to parties that owing to their identical political aims do not compete with each other in any federal state, can form a parliamentary party. The number of seats they receive in the parliamentary committees and the Council of Elders depends on the size of the parliamentary party.

Electorate
Just under 62 million Germans aged 18 or over are called on to cast a vote in the elections to the Bundestag. Women account for more than 32 million of them and thus constitute a majority of the electorate. At the 2005 general elections to the Bundestag, 2.6 million persons were enfranchised as first-time voters.

The political system

The Federal Republic of Germany is a democratic, federal and social constitutional state. Together with the basic rights, these principles form the inviolable core of the constitution, adherence to which is guarded over by the Federal Constitutional Court

appoints

Federal Government
The executive consists of the Federal Chancellor and the Federal Ministers. Each minister is personally responsible for managing the ministry in question in line with the guidelines

proposes ministers

Federal Chancellor
He forms the cabinet and is the head of government. He issues the guidelines for politics and bears the responsibility for government

elects

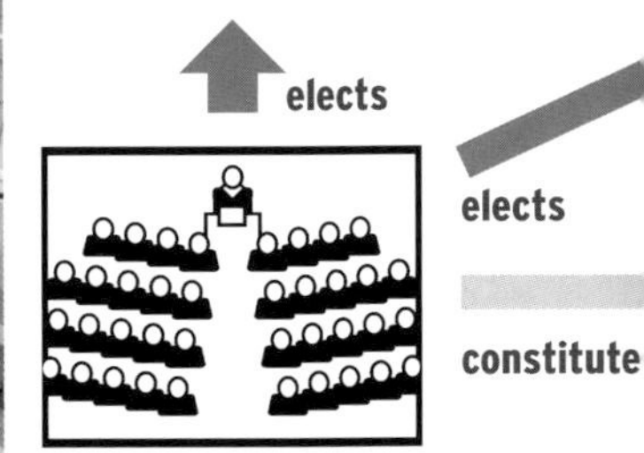

elects

constitute

Bundestag
The parliament is elected for four years and is made up of 598 members. Depending on the election result there can be "overhang seats". Its central tasks are to pass legislation and control government

The German Federal Chancellors

1. **Konrad Adenauer (CDU)** 1949-1963
2. **Ludwig Erhard (CDU)** 1963-1966
3. **Kurt Georg Kiesinger (CDU)** 1966-1969
4. **Willy Brandt (SPD)** 1969-1974
5. **Helmut Schmidt (SPD)** 1974-1982
6. **Helmut Kohl (CDU)** 1982-1998
7. **Gerhard Schröder (SPD)** 1998-2005
8. **Angela Merkel (CDU)** since 2005

The German Bundestag's plenary auditorium

vote

Electorate
All German citizens over the age of 18 have the right to vote. They vote for members of parliament in general, direct, free, equal and secret elections

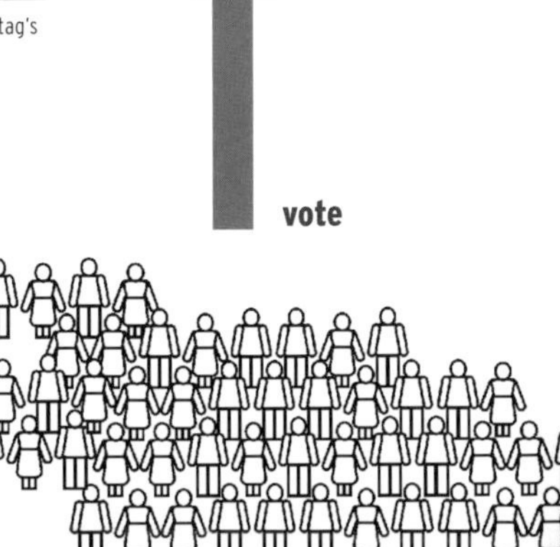

Schloss Bellevue, the official seat of the Federal President

Federal President
He is the head of state of the Federal Republic of Germany The Federal President primarily discharges representative functions and represents the Federal Republic inside and outside the country

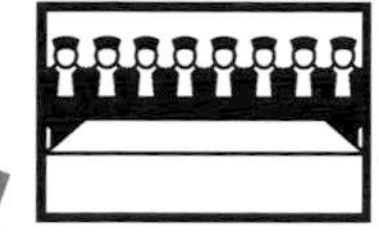

Federal Constitutional Court
The country's supreme court consists of 16 judges. Half of them are voted for by the Bundestag, the other half by the Bundesrat. They can only be elected for one term of office

elects for 5 years

elects

Federal Convention
This elects the Federal President and is made up of the members of the Bundestag and an equal number of persons elected by the state parliaments

Bundesrat
Its 69 members are delegates of the state governments and participate in the legislative process. They represent the states' interests at the federal level

constitute

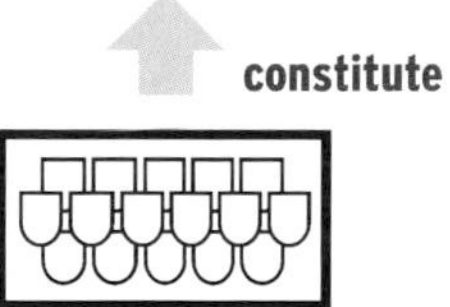

constitute

State parliaments
The members of the state parliaments are voted directly, they enact laws and control the governments

State governments
The governments of the federal states are made up of a Minister President and the state ministries. The way the governments are formed and their scope differs from state to state

vote

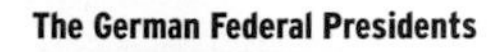

The German Federal Presidents

1. **Theodor Heuss (FDP)** 1949-1959
2. **Heinrich Lübke (CDU)** 1959-1969
3. **Gustav Heinemann (SPD)** 1969-1974
4. **Walter Scheel (FDP)** 1974-1979
5. **Karl Carstens (CDU)** 1979-1984
6. **Richard v. Weizsäcker (CDU)** 1984-1994
7. **Roman Herzog (CDU)** 1994-1999
8. **Johannes Rau (SPD)** 1999-2004
9. **Horst Köhler (CDU)** since 2004

Electoral system
The German electoral system is based on slightly modified, i.e., so-called personalized, proportional representation. Each voter has two votes, the first of which is for a candidate in his or her constituency, the second for a state list of candidates put up by a particular party. The number of seats a party holds in the Bundestag is determined by the number of valid second votes it receives.

Assembly for the people's representatives: the Bundestag auditorium

Five-percent threshold
Only those parties are taken into account when allocating seats in the Bundestag as have overcome the following hurdle: they must have polled at least five percent of the vote or won at least three constituencies outright.

democratic party. It was initially only successful in the five eastern states of the Federal Republic, which until 1990 had formed the GDR. In the 2005 general election, candidates from the newly founded party named Wahlalternative Arbeit & Soziale Gerechtigkeit (WASG, Electoral Alternative Labor and Social Justice) which had hitherto only challenged in a state election, were included on the PDS list, which renamed itself The Left Party.PDS. In June 2007, the two parties joined to form the party The Left Party.

The electoral system

The German **electoral system** makes it very difficult for any one party to form a government on its own. This has only happened once in 56 years. An alliance of parties is the general rule. So that voters know which partner the party they voted for is considering governing with, the parties issue coalition statements before embarking on the election campaign. By voting for a particular party citizens thus express on the one hand a preference for a specific party alliance, and on the other determine the balance of power between the desired future partners in government.

The Bundestag

The Bundestag is the elected representation of the German people. Technically speaking half the 598 seats in the Bundestag are allocated by means of the parties' state lists (the second vote) and the other half by the direct election of candidates in the 299 constituencies (the first vote). This division changes nothing with regard to the key role of the parties in the electoral system. Only those candidates who belong to a party have any chance of success. The party to whom members of the Bundestag belong is meant to reflect the distribution of votes. In order to prevent complications in the formation of majorities by the presence of small and very small parties a **five-percent threshold** is designed to stop their being represented in the Bundestag.

The Bundestag is the German parliament. Its elected representatives are organized in parliamentary parties and select a President from among them. It is the function of the Bundestag to elect the Federal Chancellor and keep him in office through support for his policies. The **members of parliament** can relieve the Chancellor of his duties by denying him their confidence, as do other parliaments. Nor does it make any great difference that in Germany the Chancellor is elected, whereas in Great Britain and other parliamentary democracies he is appointed by the head of state. In other parliamentary democracies, a party leader who can rely on a parliamentary majority is always appointed head of government.

The second major function of the elected representatives in the Bundestag is to pass legislation. Since 1949 some 9,000 bills have been introduced to Parliament and more than 6200 laws enacted. These were predominantly amendments to existing acts. Most drafts are tabled by the Federal Government. A small number are introduced by Parliament or the Bundesrat. Here, again, the Bundestag is similar to parliaments in other parliamentary democracies in that it for the most part enacts bills proposed by the Federal Government. The Bundestag, however, is less like the debating parliament typified by British parliamentary culture and corresponds more closely to a working parliament.

Members of parliament

Members of the German Bundestag are voted for in general, direct, free, equal and secret elections. They are representatives of the entire nation and are not tied to orders and instructions. Exclusion or resignation from a party therefore does not affect their status as members of the Bundestag. In practice, however, membership of a party plays a decisive role, as the members of one and the same party, to the extent that they hold the requisite minimum number of seats, form parliamentary parties, and these shape the face of parliamentary activities.

The 16th German Bundestag

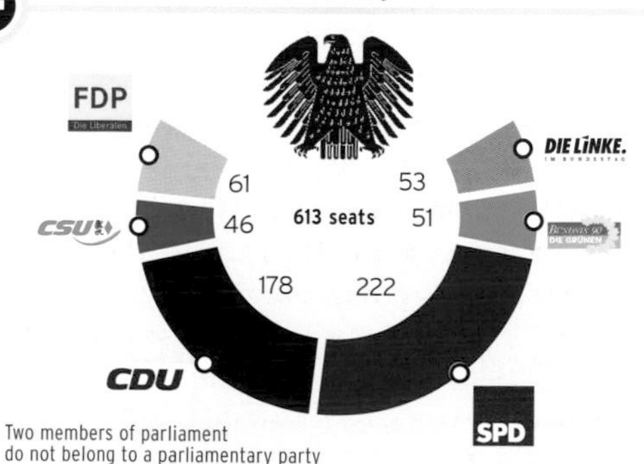

Two members of parliament do not belong to a parliamentary party

On September 18 2005 the 16th German Bundestag was elected. The election had been preceded by the dissolution of the Bundestag following a failed vote of confidence in the Federal Chancellor. The new Parliament is made up of five parliamentary parties. The SPD, the CDU and CSU together form a grand coalition government. The President of the Bundestag – and thus the second-highest ranking official in the country – is the CDU member of parliament Norbert Lammert. Women make up 32 percent of the members of parliament.

Parliamentary Committees
The Bundestag's Committees are bodies answerable to the entire parliament. In the 16th legislative period, the parliament convened 22 standing committees. The constitution stipulates that a Foreign Affairs Committee, an EU Committee, a Defense and a Petitions Committee be established. Their duties are to prepare the debates before the Bundestag. In the presence of representatives of the government and the Bundesrat, draft bills are examined and differences of opinion between the government and the opposition overcome wherever possible.

The Bundestag's expert **Parliamentary Committees** discuss the bills introduced to Parliament in great detail. Here, the activities of the Bundestag resemble to some extent Congress in the USA, the prototype of a working parliament.

The third major function of the Bundestag is to keep a check on the government's work. It is the opposition that fulfills the function of monitoring the work of government in a manner visible to the general public. A less evident, but no less effective form of control is carried out by the elected representatives of the governing parties, who behind closed doors ask the government representatives critical questions.

The Federal President

The Federal President is the head of state of the Federal Republic of Germany. He represents the country in its dealings with other countries and appoints government members, judges and high-ranking civil servants. With his signature, acts become legally binding. He can dismiss the government and, in exceptional cases, dissolve parliament before its term of office is completed. The Basic Law does not accord the Federal President a right of veto such as is held by the President of the United States and other state presidents. Though the Federal President confirms parliamentary decisions and government proposals with regard to ministers, he only checks whether they have come about by the due procedure in accordance with the Basic Law.

The Head of State: Federal President Horst Köhler represents Germany – to the outside world, too. Pictured here on a trip to Africa

The Federal President remains in office for a period of five years; he can be re-elected only once. He is elected by the Federal Convention, which is made up of members of the Bundestag, on the one hand, and by an equal number of members selected by parliaments of the 16 federal states, on the other.

The Federal Chancellor and the government

The Federal Chancellor is the only member of the **Federal Government** to be elected. The constitution empowers him to

Central coordination agency for the government's policies: The Federal Chancellery on the bank of the River Spree in Berlin

personally choose his ministers, who head the most important political authorities. Moreover it is the Chancellor who determines the number of ministries and their responsibilities. It is he who lays down the guidelines of government policy. These outline the Chancellor's right to stipulate binding government activities. This authority gives the Federal Chancellor a whole array of instruments of leadership that easily stands up to a comparison with the power of the President in a presidential democracy.

The Parliamentary Council, which in 1949 resolved the Basic Law, took as its role model for the Federal Chancellor the position of the Prime Minister in Great Britain. The Prime Minister possesses exactly the same means of power as that of Chancellor, though the latter's power is actually far less than that of the British premier. In the British parliamentary system only one party is ever in power, because the first-past-the-post system there favors the strongest party. As a rule, in the Bundestag no one party has a clear majority. For this reason a **coalition**, in other words an alliance of various parties is normally necessary to be able to elect a Chancellor. The election of the Chancellor is preceded by extensive negotiations between those parties that plan to govern together. These address specific topics such as how the ministries are to be divided up between the parties,

Federal Government
The Federal Government and cabinet is made up of the Federal Chancellor and the Federal Ministers. While the Chancellor holds the power to issue directives, the ministers have departmental powers, meaning that they independently run their respective ministries in the framework of those directives. Moreover, the cabinet abides by the collegial principle, in disputes the Federal Government decides by majority. The affairs of state are managed by the Chancellor.

Coalitions
Since the first elections to the Bundestag in 1949 there have been 21 coalition governments in Germany. Durable alliances were, for example, the Social Democrat/Liberal coalition which ran from 1969 until 1982, the CDU/CSU and FDP coalition, which ran from 1982 to 1998, and the Social Democrat/Green alliances which endured from 1998 to 2005. A grand coalition of CDU/CSU and SPD is currently in power in Germany.

Federal Chancellor
The Federal Chancellor is elected by the Bundestag after being proposed by the Federal President. The Federal Chancellor then proposes to the Federal President which ministers should be appointed/dismissed. The Federal Chancellor heads the Federal Government in keeping with rules of procedure authorized by the Federal President. He bears responsibility for the Government vis-à-vis the Bundestag and in the case of national defense is supreme commander of the German Armed Forces.

which ministries are to be maintained and which newly created. The strongest party in the alliance is accorded the right to propose the **Federal Chancellor**. In addition the parties agree on the policies they intend to tackle in the next few years. The results of these coalition negotiations are enshrined in the coalition treaty. Only when these steps have been completed is the Chancellor elected. Negotiations between the government parties prepare the decisions taken by the Federal Government and accompany them afterwards. Should there no longer be political consensus between the parties before general elections for a new Bundestag are due, removing the Chancellor from office becomes an alternative. Should a constructive vote of no confidence result in the current Chancellor indeed being removed from office, a new Chancellor must be elected at the same time. This repeal of parliamentary confidence forces the parties represented in the Bundestag to form a new, functioning government majority before they bring down the Chancellor. There have only been two previous attempts to bring down the Chancellor, only one of which succeeded, namely in 1982 when a vote of no confidence was passed against the Chancellor Helmut Schmidt (SPD), who was replaced by Helmut Kohl (CDU).

One of the most frequented buildings in Germany: The Reichstag, seat of the German Bundestag

However, at any time the Federal Chancellor himself can also propose a vote of no confidence in the Bundestag to test whether he still enjoys the unlimited support of the governing parties. Should the Chancellor lose the vote this indicates that parts of the government majority are drifting away from the Chancellor, leaving the Federal President to decide whether the Bundestag should be dissolved and a general election held. The Federal President can also request the parties represented in the Bundestag to try and form a new government.

In the history of the Federal Republic there has never been a genuine defeat in a vote of no confidence. There have on three occasions been previously arranged defeats: The elected representatives of the government parties or the ministers abstained in order to bring down the government in 1972, 1982, and 2005. This course of action was taken in order to prematurely dissolve the Bundestag, which according to the constitution is otherwise not possible. It can only be taken with the approval of the Federal President and is not uncontroversial. As early as 1983 the Constitutional Court stressed that this was a questionable process not in keeping with the intentions of Constitution. In 2005, an appeal was again made to the supreme court, but in this case the constitutional judges again rejected the petitions of two elected representatives of the Bundestag.

The Basic Law as a work of art: Installation by Dani Karavan near the Reichstag building

The federal structure

The German federal state is a complex entity. It consists of a central Federal Government and 16 federal states. The Basic Law lays out in great detail which issues fall within the ambit of the Federal Government and which devolve to the federal states. As such the federal system in Germany is similar to that of other federal countries. Public life in Germany is predominantly based on central laws. In accordance with the **principle of subsidiarity** citizens, on the other hand, deal almost exclusively with state and local authorities acting on behalf of the federal states. The reason for this is the aim of the Basic Law to combine the advantages of a unified state with those of a federal state. In everyday life citizens of other countries have far more frequent dealings with representatives of central government.

Principle of subsidiarity
Subsidiarity is a core concept in a federal structure. According to it, the smallest unit of the social community capable of handling problems shall bear responsibility and take the decisions – starting from the individual and working upwards via the family, associations and local authorities to the states, the nation as a whole, and the European Union and the United Nations.

The Basic Law stipulates that it be possible to compare living conditions throughout Germany. Essentially these are determined by economic and social policy. For this reason central laws mainly regulate this particular field. To this extent the German federal state resembles a centralized state. Nonetheless it is the federal states that control the major part of pan-state administration. This means that federalist elements dominate the state administrative systems. First, as is typical of a federal state, its own administrative system enforces the laws that apply in that particular state. In addition they also execute most central laws, which is untypical of federal state systems. As such, formulations such as "unitarian" are used to characterize the German federal state.

There are three pan-state functions that the individual federal states exercise on their own: schooling (to a large extent tertiary education, too), internal security (including policing) as well as the organization of **local self-government**. Thanks to the wide-ranging rights pertaining to guaranteed participation they enjoy in the Bundesrat, the federal states receive a form of compensation for the fact that central government is the primary body determining legislation.

Local self-government
According to the Basic Law, the cities, municipalities and districts have the right themselves to regulate local affairs within the framework of the law. This right of self-administration specifically covers public local transport, public road-building, water, gas and electricity supplies, sewage disposal services and town planning

Participation in the legislative process: Bundesrat plenary session

The Bundesrat

The Bundesrat represents the federal states and alongside the Bundestag is a form of Second Chamber. It is obliged to deliberate on each federal law. As the chamber of the federal states, the Bundesrat has the same function as those Second Chambers in other federal states that are mostly referred to as the Senate. The Bundesrat is made up exclusively of representatives of the federal state governments. The number of votes each state holds is aligned in a sense to the size of its population: Each state has at least three, and

Distribution of seats in the Bundesrat

The Bundesrat is one of the five permanent constitutional bodies in the Federal Republic of Germany. It is involved in the legislative process and thus takes part in Federal decision-making and in European Union matters. Its 69 members are delegates of the 16 state governments. The votes each state has depends on the size of its respective population. Each state can only vote unanimously. The office of President of the Bundesrat is held for one year by the Minister President of each state; the sequence is determined by the size of the states' respective populations.

those with the highest populations up to six. Bremen, the smallest state has a mere 660,000 inhabitants, the largest, North Rhine-Westphalia over 18 million.

The Bundesrat plays a part in the passing of federal legislation. Here, it differs from the Second Chamber of other federal states. The Basic Law envisages two forms of participation. Central laws that cause the federal states additional administrative costs or replace existing central laws require the approval of the Bundesrat: The latter is required to endorse laws passed by the Bundestag for these to become legally binding. In this regard, the Bundesrat enjoys the same rights as the Bundestag in terms of being a legislative organ. Currently more than 50 percent of all laws passed require the approval of the Bundesrat. Since federal laws are in principle enforced by the administrative bodies of the federal states, the most important and most costly laws involve the administrative sovereignty of the federal states. A difference should be made between these approval laws and the appeal laws.

The link between the Federal Government and the federal states: The Bundesrat in the former Preussisches Herrenhaus at the heart of Berlin

The legal system

The Federal Republic of Germany is a democratic constitutional state that guarantees stable laws, the protection of liberties, and equality before the law. This is essentially ensured by the Basic Law, as the principles of a democratic constitutional state are enshrined in the constitution. The German supreme court, namely the Federal Constitutional Court monitors maintenance of these rights and the preservation of justice.
In Germany, the administration of justice is divided into five branches: ordinary, labor, administrative, social and financial courts. In a normal case there are three higher tiers that can re-assess court decisions. The plaintiffs and the accused can appeal against a court ruling.

Thereupon the litigation goes before a "higher" court and a ruling is handed down. Not until the third level has been reached is there no longer any right of appeal and the litigation thus comes to an end.
Justice is passed down by some 21,000 independent judges who are bound only to the law and are, as a rule, appointed for life. They may not on principle be removed from office. Moreover, there are some 5,000 public prosecutors in Germany and more than 100,000 lawyers.
In surveys on political and legal stability, foreign investors put Germany second only to Great Britain. This legal stability attracts foreign companies and is to the benefit of investments and entrepreneurial activity in Germany.

Federal Constitutional Court
This is based in Karlsruhe and consists of two senates, each with eight judges, one half of whom is elected by the Bundestag, the other half voted by the Bundesrat. Each judge is appointed for 12 years and is not eligible for re-election.

Though the Bundesrat can reject the latter, the Bundestag can overrule the objection with the same majority as in the Bundesrat – a simple, an absolute or a two-thirds majority.

If one considers that the activities of the Bundesrat are spread across the shoulders of the 16 state governments, it becomes clear that the federal state governments are important players in the nation-wide political arena. For this reason, the state prime ministers, being the heads of the federal state governments, are known far beyond the borders of their own individual states. Since September 2006, the **reform of the federal system** has recalibrated the respective scope of central government and of the individual federal states. The goal of the reform: to improve the decision-making abilities and scope for action of both central government and the federal state governments, and to more clearly assign political responsibilities.

The Federal Constitutional Court

The **Federal Constitutional Court** is a characteristic institution of post-war German democracy. The Basic Law accorded it the right to repeal legislation passed as part of the legitimate democratic process should it come to the conclusion that such legislation contravenes the Basic Law. The Constitutional Court only acts in response to petitions. Those entitled to lodge a complaint include the federal bodies Federal President, Bundestag, Bundesrat, Federal Government and their constituent parts – elected representatives or parliamentary

The topic on the Internet

www.bundespraesident.de
This Web site provides information on the person and office of the Federal President and publishes speeches and interviews (English, French, German, Spanish)

www.bundestag.de
The Bundestag Web site describes the parliamentary parties and MPs, and offers access to Web casts of debates (English, French, German)

www.bundesrat.de
Daily agendas and parliamentary printed matter are to be found on this home page alongside extensive information on the work of the Bundesrat (English, French, German)

www.bundesverfassungsgericht.de
In addition to general data, all verdicts since 1998 by the Federal Constitutional Court can be downloaded from its Website (German, English)

www.bundesregierung.de
This portal is a source of information about the most important political topics (English, French, German)

parties – as well as federal state governments. In "constitution-related" disputes, the Constitutional Court acts to protect the division of powers guaranteed in the Basic Law and the federal state. In order to enable parliamentary minorities to be able to appeal to the Constitutional Court, one third of the elected representatives of the Bundestag is sufficient to submit a complaint against a valid law ("abstract judicial review").

Furthermore, the Basic Law empowers individual citizens to launch a "constitutional complaint" should they feel that the state has infringed their basic rights. Year after year thousands of citizens register a complaint against the constitution. However, the Court reserves the right to select from the mass of petitions submitted only those that can be expected to result in verdicts that point the way ahead in terms of the validity of basic rights. Ultimately every German court is obliged to submit a petition for actual assessment of the normative basis to the Constitutional Court should it consider a law to be un-constitutional. The Federal Constitutional Court holds a monopoly on interpretation of the constitution with regard to all jurisdiction.

Germany and Europe

Germany shares the same basic features of its political system with most members of the European Union (EU). Its system of government is one of parliamentary democracy, in other words, government policy is determined by the head of government and the ministers, and not by the head of state. Given the high standards with regard to the constitutional state and democracy as a result of the Basic Law, the Federal Constitutional Court is also a player in the European political arena. The court has illustrated on several occasions that European law must satisfy the criteria of the Basic Law if Germany is to relinquish to the EU the rights to draw up its own laws. In this respect to a certain extent the "eternal guarantee" of applicable principles with regard to the Basic Law vie with the Basic Law's commitment to European integration. ●

Reform of the federal system
Since September 1, 2006 provisions concerning reform of the federal system have been in place. The most comprehensive reform to the Basic Law since 1949 enhances the ability of both the Federation and the states to take decisions and to make the division of political powers clearer. This reform reduces the number of federal laws requiring the consent of the Bundesrat from about 60 percent to 35-40 percent. At the same time, however, some powers have been transferred to the states, above all as regards education policy. The Federation also gained powers in the fields of environmental policy and waste management.

Jürgen Hartmann
Professor Jürgen Hartmann lectures in Political Sciences at the German Armed Forces Helmut Schmidt University in Hamburg. He has authored countless textbooks and introductions to various areas of political science.

5

Foreign policy

In the age of globalization, foreign policy is, more than ever before, the world's domestic policy. States, societies and economic zones are all becoming networked. The end of the East-West conflict has opened up new opportunities for German foreign policy - both within Europe and worldwide. Germany has accepted the international responsibility that has evolved for the country in the wake of dramatic changes with regard to world politics, and, together with its European and transatlantic partners, is deeply committed to the causes of democracy, human rights and the dialog between cultures. The prime objective of Germany's foreign policy is to maintain peace and safety in the world.

Germany – a partner worldwide

By Gregor Schöllgen

THE 20TH CENTURY WAS characterized by quite unprecedented disruption. Three global conflicts, namely the two World Wars and the Cold War as well as a series of revolutionary upheavals left a deep mark on nations and peoples alike. This is especially true of Germany, if only because the country at the heart of Europe was both responsible for the developments that led to the outbreak of both world wars and was affected to an unusual degree by the Cold War and the gradual dissolution of the bipolar world order at the end of the 1980s.

When the old order collapsed, Germany faced a new situation as regards domestic and foreign policy. Here, the country benefited from the dynamism that culminated in the disbandment of the Soviet Union at the end of 1991. For this led not just to the unification of East and West Germany, but also for the first time in almost 50 years to complete sovereignty.

For united Germany, a new era of exceptional challenges began. First, the new domestic situation had to be mastered and second there was a new, unusual role to be played in **foreign policy**. The expectations associated with Germany were great precisely because the country had profited from global trends and achieved its express goal with unification. This was as true of its longstanding allies as it was of both the former members of the Eastern bloc, and the peoples and countries of the Southern hemisphere, which since the end of the 20th century has been undergoing emphatic transformation. It was likewise no coinci-

Foreign policy
The primary goal of German foreign policy is to preserve peace and security in the world. The expanded concept of security covers not only questions of conflict prevention, defense, disarmament and arms controls, but also economic, ecological and social issues as well as human rights. This includes a committed effort on behalf of human rights world-wide and a global economy that creates opportunities for everyone, of fostering cross-border environmental protection and an open dialog between the cultures. Foreign cultural and education policy forms an integral part of German foreign policy. Its practical implementation is largely handled by intermediary agency organizations such as the Goethe-Institut, the German Academic Exchange Service (DAAD), the Alexander von Humboldt Foundation, the Institute for Foreign Cultural Relations (ifa) and the German UNESCO Commission (see page 162).

Cooperation at the United Nations: Federal Foreign Minister Frank-Walter Steinmeier with UN Secretary General Ban Ki-moon

dence that these peoples and nations looked to Germany. The German Reich had lost all its colonies in World War I, and after World War II no people in Asia, Africa or the Pacific rim thus had to struggle with East or West Germany to obtain independence.

Fundamentals of German foreign policy

As a result, united Germany found itself back at the center of the world political stage almost overnight. This realignment was successful thanks to the **fundamentals of German foreign policy** as had firmly evolved since the foundation of the Federal Republic of Germany. One of the key features of Germany's political culture has always been its focus on a broad consensus on foreign policy issues and on maintaining continuity in specific areas.

Since the days of Germany's first Federal Chancellor Konrad Adenauer these have included the **Transatlantic partnership** and European integration, the wish for good neighborly relations – primarily with France, something German foreign policy has sought to achieve since the early 1950s – and the difficult process of reconciliation with Israel, which Germany commenced at an early date. This may sound obvious, but against the backdrop of German policy, war-waging during the first half of the 20th century, and the rigid Cold War, but was far from easy. As of the end of the 1960s, in particular since Willy Brandt's chancellorship (1969–1974), the westward focus has been supplemented and advanced by a policy of conciliation with Poland and the other countries of East and Eastern Central Europe. Indeed, Germany is now allied with Russia in a strategic partnership.

The bedrock of German foreign policy, as steadily created by all the different Federal Governments, has been the country's comprehensive integration into multilateral cooperation. This was fostered after the experience of two world wars by the unequivocal will of the country's neighbors to include and control it, and thus deter the Germans

Fundamentals of foreign policy
German foreign policy comes under the sign of continuity and reliability. It is shaped by cooperation in a spirit of partnership and a wish to balance interests. The key parameters of German foreign policy can be described by the twin lodestars of "never again" and "never alone". "Never again" is to be seen against the background of German history and understood as a rejection of authoritarian and expansion-oriented politics as well as profound skepticism against the means of military power. "Never alone" signifies Germany's firm embedding in the community of Western democracies. Germany's integration into a Europe that is growing ever more closely together and its firm roots in the North Atlantic Treaty Organization comprise the cornerstones of its orientation in foreign policy. Germany is involved in many ways in organizations for multilateral cooperation.

from breaking out or going it alone; and it was also fostered by the Germans' elementary need for peace, security, prosperity and democracy, as well as the recognition that the integration of their country formed the basis for its unification.

History proved them right, and it is thus no coincidence that after the end of the Cold War precisely the Germans focused on those international organizations that had already given the "old" Federal Republic support, namely the European Union (EU), the North Atlantic Treaty Organization (NATO), the United Nations (UN), and the Conference on Security and Cooperation in Europe (CSCE). However, these alliances were shaped by the Cold War, in other words by a past era. While the organizations of the communist world dissolved in 1991 and the CSCE was renamed the Organization for Security and Cooperation in Europe (OSCE), since the end of the Cold War the West and the United Nations have faced the need for reform.

Transatlantic partnership
The Transatlantic partnership forms the basis of German and European security. A close and trusting relationship to the United States continues to be of outstanding importance for Germany's security. However, the Transatlantic partnership is far more than a purely political and military alliance. The close links to the United States have a strong history, rest on shared cultural roots, and are an expression of a profound community of values and interests.

International peace operations

Germany is engaged in finding solutions to international conflicts and promoting civil societies in several locations throughout the world. Both as a member of multilateral forces and at the national level Germany makes great efforts to improve the arsenal of crisis prevention instruments. These include United Nations' peace-keeping missions as well as projects that assist the process of democratization and the posting of civil personnel. In 2002, the Federal Foreign Office in Berlin founded the Center for International Peace Operations (ZIF) with the aim of specifically preparing civilian helpers for international operations organized by the UN, the OSCE and the European Union. A swift response by Germany to crises and conflicts in the form of armed operations on the part of the German Armed Forces (Bundeswehr) occurs only in collaboration with allies and partners as part of a NATO, EU or UN operation. In June 2007, there were more than 8,000 German troops on active international peace-keeping missions.

The spectrum ranges from the fight against terrorism as part of "Enduring Freedom" in the Horn of Africa to peace-keeping missions in the Balkans (KFOR, EUFOR) and Afghanistan (ISAF), German Armed Forces operations in Sudan as part of the UNMIS Observation Mission, to humanitarian aid. Since the first deployment of German forces in Cambodia in 1992, 200,000 German troops have been involved in the preservation of peace and stability in crisis regions.

www.bundeswehr.de

The Crisis Response Center in the Federal Foreign Office organizes help, provides information, and coordinates matters

Security Council
December 2004 saw the end of Germany's fourth term as an elected member of the UN Security Council since it joined the United Nations in 1973. In order to adjust the United Nations to the new political realities, in the context of a comprehensive reform of the organization Germany advocates expanding the Security Council and ensuring its deliberations are even more transparent.

Foreign policy in the age of globalization

Germany is one of the advocates of appropriate reform to the international organizations, for which there are good reasons: First, no other comparable country is so embedded in multilateral political, economic and military cooperation.

Second, German foreign policy takes into account the far greater international responsibility which Germany now has at the request of the world community: In this context Germany is pushing for a comprehensive reform of the UN's organizational structures, including a wish for a permanent seat in the **Security Council**.

Moreover, for German foreign policy the formation of an independent identity for European security constitutes a key side to strengthening the European pillar of NATO. When in December 2004 NATO transferred leadership of the troops (which have since operated as EUFOR) in Bosnia-Herzegovina to the **ESDP** (European Security and Defense Policy) and the Europeans thus for the first time endeavored to control a flashpoint using their own financing and resources, this marked a new stage in the transformation of the transatlantic alliance. The responsibility

Involvement in international organizations

European Union

Since 1957 Germany has been one of the six founding members of today's EU. Since 2007, it has consisted of 27 member states and the euro is the official tender in 15 of them. Germany contributes EUR 22.1 billion to the EU budget of EUR 115.5 billion (2007). Günter Verheugen is Vice-President of the European Commission responsible for Enterprise and Industry. **www.eu.int**

United Nations

The United Nations was founded in 1945 with the goal of safeguarding world peace. With 192 member states, almost all the countries in the world belong to the UN. Germany has been a member since 1973 and following the United States and Japan is the third largest contributor to the UN budget. Since 1996, Germany has been one of the UN countries that is home to UN institutions; among others, the UNFCCC Climate Change Secretariat has been based in Bonn. **www.un.org**

NATO

The North Atlantic Treaty Organization was founded in 1949. Today, this defense alliance has 26 member states; Germany joined in 1955. The German Armed Forces have since March 1999 been part of NATO's mission in Kosovo, with 2,230 soldiers stationed there at year-end 2007, and 3,140 soldiers on the NATO-led operation in Afghanistan. NATO's HQ is in Brussels; its highest body is the NATO Council. **www.nato.int**

that the European Union is willing to assume in the Balkans can also be gauged from the fact that its has committed a 1,800-strong international civil EULEX mission to Kosovo, designed to contribute to establishing rule-of law structures there.

The Federal Government first made use of its new scope for foreign policy as a unified state since 1990 after the turn of the millennium: The German statement on the terrorist attacks of September 11 2001 was not only prompt, Chancellor Gerhard Schröder went further than any of his predecessors and promised America Germany's "unconditional solidarity".

Needless to say, the Federal Government also supported the decision by NATO on October 2, 2001 to invoke for the first time in its history Article 5 of its charter. The subsequent deployment of German soldiers to the Hindukush had a political side: the Bonn Conference on Afghanistan and the agreements reached there on the legal and political basis for a transitional government for Afghanistan. And it had a military side: since January 2002, the German Armed Forces have made a strong contribution to **ISAF**, the International Security Assistance Force for Afghanistan.

ESDP/CFSP

A common approach in the field of foreign and defense policy is expected to enable the EU member states to respond more swiftly to international crises and conflicts, to speak with a single voice in terms of foreign policy and more effectively assert its international interests. In the framework of the Common Foreign & Security Policy (CFSP), the EU has developed a common European Security and Defense policy (ESDP). The member states provide up to 60,000 troops within 60 days for humanitarian tasks, rescue missions, peace-keeping measures and combat. Since January 2007, each half-year two "battle groups" (RDFs) of about 1,500 soldiers each are ready for deployment.

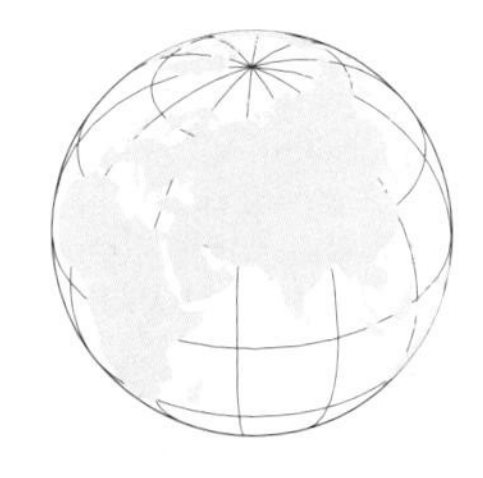

OSCE

With its 56 member states, the Organization for Organization and Co-Operation in Europe (OSCE) is a comprehensive forum for cooperation at the pan-European level. OSCE missions are active above all in conflict prevention and management. Germany makes a substantial contribution to finance and man-power.
www.osce.org

WTO

The World Trade Organization (WTO) was founded in 1995 and serves to implement the existing treaties on international trade. It is likewise a forum for negotiation on liberalizing global trade. In the present Doha round Germany has been expressly championing better integration of the developing countries into world trade.
www.wto.org

IMF

The key task of the International Monetary Fund (IMF) in Washington, D.C., is to promote the macroeconomic stability of its 185 member states. Germany's capital quota is 6.0 percent, making it one of the key IMF members; through a German executive director it also participates in IMF decision-making.
www.imf.org

NATO – central forum for security and cooperation

ISAF
Originally, the deployment of the International Security Assistance Force for Afghanistan was a military operation. With its rulings of April 1993 and June 1994 the Federal Constitutional Court in Karlsruhe cleared the path for deployment by the German Armed Forces on such missions; since December 2004 the Act on Parliamentary Participation on Decisions to Deploy Armed Forces Abroad sets out the Bundestag's powers in such cases. Today, under a UN mandate the ISAF supports the Government of Afghanistan in providing and maintaining a secure environment and facilitating the reconstruction of the country.

Gregor Schöllgen
The Professor of Modern and Contemporary History at the University of Erlangen-Nuremberg has been visiting professor in Oxford, New York and the London School of Economics.

In total, this century up to 10,000 German soldiers have been posted on international missions – despite the fact that the German Armed Forces have by no means completed their transformation from a territorial army to a flexible deployment force. These wide-ranging responsibilities were also a key argument when it came to justifying why Germany did not take part in the campaign in Iraq in 2003. The fact that German foreign policy took this situation into account and set sovereign priorities sheds some light on the country's new role.

German foreign policy also promotes introducing civil society structures; it is committed to helping overcome natural disasters, asserting democratic and human rights, and to the war on terror. In fact, Germany also uses its new role to secure human rights, peace, and dialog – both in the Middle East and elsewhere.

The fact that Germany can live this role stems from the trust carefully nurtured over the decades. German politics is measured not against the yardstick of the destructive apparatus of the Third Reich, but against its achievements in development and integration. And here Germany has demonstrated that it knows how to assume such responsibilities. ●

Germany in Europe

By Josef Janning

Germany and Europe: Integration in a united Europe is anchored in the Basic Law

CAN A COUNTRY THAT SHARES BORDERS on all sides with other European countries, namely Germany with its nine neighbors, afford not to actively pursue a European policy? The answer is self-evident: With its central location at the heart of today's European Union (EU) the Germans have a special interest in living in peace and harmony with their neighbors. As the EU member state with the largest population, a strong economy and central geographical position, united Germany has an overriding interest in being closely included in the development and advancement of European integration and its future expansion.

It is in Germany's interest for Europe to be a vibrant continent. In the past, the integration process has proved to be a suitable basis for ensuring peace, prosperity and security. By means of common policy, Germany has forged firm links to partners who are its neighbors and with Europe it has

Development policy

German development policy as a constituent part of a global structural and peace policy endeavors to improve living conditions in partner countries. It concentrates on creating social justice, enhancing economic output and achieving political stability through peace, human rights, democracy, and equal rights.

A key objective is to protect the environment. The guidelines and concepts underlying German development policy are devised by the Federal Ministry for Economic Cooperation and Development (BMZ), which collaborates with some 70 partner countries. Africa is a focal region as there the greatest efforts are required to realize the Millennium Development Goals. During its presidency of both the Council of the European Union and the G8 in 2007, Germany succeeded in ensuring partnership with Africa was accorded a central place both in the EU and the G8. That said, Germany will continue to support other regions, such as Latin America.

Germany adheres to the commitments and goals of the United Nation's Millennium Declaration, the Monterrey Consensus and the Johannesburg Plan of Implementation. By the year 2010, Germany therefore intends to devote at least 0.51 percent of gross domestic product and by 2015 as much as 0.7 percent to overseas development aid.

www.bmz.de

European integration
The European unification process is one of the major keystones of German foreign policy. The participation of the Federal Republic in a united Europe is anchored in the Basic Law. With the accession of Bulgaria and Romania in 2007, the European Union has grown to 27 member states. Accession negotiations have started with Turkey and Croatia. The Former Yugoslav Republic of Macedonia is an official accession candidate, while the other Western Balkan states are potential candidates.

both once again achieved unification and also gained respect and a voice in the world. For the Germans, the peaceful balancing of interests with its neighbors and the world has thus become the recipe for success in European integration, the importance of which was re-emphasized by the German Presidency of the Council of the European Union in first-half 2007. Federal Chancellor Merkel and Foreign Minister Steinmeier skillfully used Germany's respect and trust in Europe to solve the institutional crisis. Germany laid the foundations for the Lisbon Treaty and gained the approval of all EU member states to strengthen the EU as regards its decision-making, policy formulation and institutional capabilities.

March 2007 marked the 50th anniversary of signature of the Treaty of Rome. In 1957, this treaty on establishing a European Economic Community spelled the beginning of the success story of **European integration**. As opposed to the initial steps, namely from the European Coal and Steel Community to the European Defense Community, the

Lisbon EU Reform Treaty

In December 2007, the EU heads of state and governments signed the EU Reform Treaty in Lisbon. Following ratification, the Reform Treaty is scheduled to come into force in all member states in 2009. It puts the EU on a new contractual footing and is meant to make it more democratic, transparent and efficient. The treaty envisages profound reforms. Thus, in future there will be a permanent EU president to strengthen continuity in EU action. EU resolutions will be simplified as in future many instances where a unanimous vote has hitherto been required will be abolished, with decisions by qualified majority to be extended to several dozen areas. As of 2014 EU Council decisions will in principle be taken by "double majority", meaning that 55% of member states and 65 percent of the population must be behind resolutions by the Council of Ministers. This will obtain for a transition period through 2017. The rotating chair of the Council of Ministers will be retained in the form of an 18-month team presidency made up of three member states. As of 2014, the number of commissioners will be reduced to two thirds the number of member states. Moreover, there will be a "High Representative of the Union for Foreign Affairs and Security Policy", who will be responsible for the EU's foreign affairs. The Reform Treaty also strengthens democracy and protection by basic rights by expanding the role of the European Parliament, the inclusion of the national parliaments into the European legislative process, and by making the Charter of Fundamental Rights mandatory (exemptions have been granted to Great Britain and Poland).

The bodies of the European Union

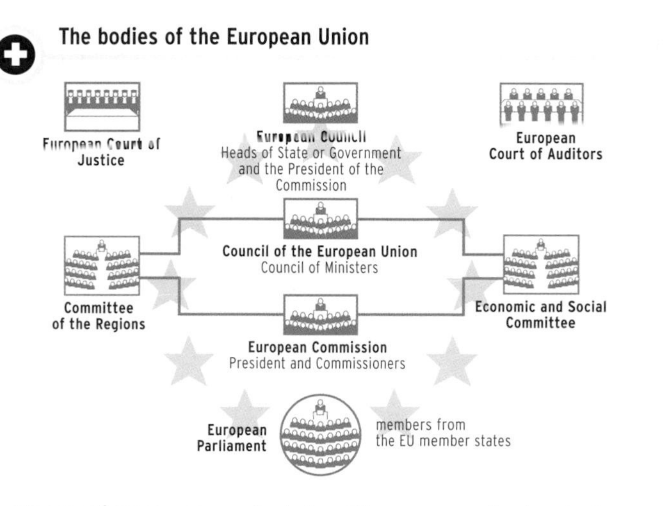

European Council
The European Council formulates the general political guidelines of the European Union. The Heads of State or Government of the member states as well as the Commission President convene in the European Council at least twice a year.

Treaty of Rome concentrated neither on monitoring industries such as coal and steel, nor on bundling defense powers. Instead, it focused on developing the economies of Western Europe by strengthening and deepening cooperation and promoting trade among the founder nations. The idea behind the resolutions of 1957 still applies today – the Treaty of Rome forms the basis of a customs union and the EU's common trade policy. The treaty thus sought to create a common market with no trade barriers. And this decision had a greater impact on the pace of European unification than any other political declaration of recent decades: The goals behind the notion of a "common market" required an authority that created a specific order – the **European Commission** as an administrative organ above the interests of individual states, as a guardian of the treaty. The treaty required the dismantling of internal borders and thus the complete freedom of goods, services, capital and labor – the program that resulted in the single European market in 1992. On this basis, it became necessary to shore these foundations up with monetary policy – this eventually led to the euro, which was introduced as legal tender in 2002.

The institutional consequences of these economic linkages stimulated the various reform stages that led to

European Commission
The European Commission is headquartered in Brussels and is a politically independent supranational body that represents and safeguards the interests of the entire EU. The EU Commission has the right to table proposals (right of initiative) for all common legal acts; as "guardian of the treaties" it ensures that common law is adhered to and in addition enjoys executive powers, for example with regard to the budget and monopolies laws. Finally it publicly represents the interests of the community. The Commission is headed by the Commission President, since 2004 José Manuel Barroso of Portugal. One of the Vice-Presidents is a German, Günter Verheugen. Each member state is represented by a Commission member. The division of commissioners' tasks follows the principle of collective responsibility – in other words: Each member is allocated certain tasks.

Stages of European unification

The over 50 years of European unification form a very special success story. It is a story that has brought durable peace and prosperity to an entire continent, where for centuries almost every nation had waged war against the others

1950
On May 9, French Foreign Minister **Robert Schuman** announced his plan to unite Europe in peace

1958
The Treaty of Rome comes into force. The EEC, EURATOM and ECSC communities have two common organs: the Court and the Parliamentary Assembly. At this time, it had 142 members and gave itself in 1962 the name of **European Parliament**

1967
The Council and Commission, until then separate entities for each of the three communities, become **united bodies**

1979
For the first time, direct elections to the **European Parliament** are held

1950 1960 1970

20th century

1951
In Paris, Belgium, the Federal Republic of Germany, France, Italy, Luxembourg and the Netherlands sign the Treaty establishing the **European Coal and Steel Community** (ECSC)

1957
In Rome, the six ECSC member states sign the Treaties establishing the **European Economic Community** (EEC) and the European Atomic Energy Community (EURATOM), which become known as the **Treaty of Rome**

1973
The number of European Community member states grows from six to nine: **Denmark, Great Britain** and **Ireland** join

1981
The Community grows southward, as **Greece** becomes a member state

1986
With the agreement on the **Single European Act**, the basis is laid for completing the single market and for the commencement of European political cooperation. The Community's enlargement southwards continues with the accession of **Spain** and **Portugal**

1992
The **Treaty of Maastricht** founds the European Union (EU). The "Community method" has since also applied to cooperation between governments of the member states in the areas of "common foreign and security policy" as well as "justice and home affairs"

1995
The EU grows to have 15 members with the accession of **Austria, Finland** and **Sweden**

1999
The **euro** is officially introduced as a currency of deposit in 11 member states, and in 2002 is launched as legal tender. In May, the **Treaty of Amsterdam** comes into force, renewing and appreciably expanding the ambit of the European Parliament

2001
With the **Nice Treaty**, the European Union laid the basis for the accession of ten further member states. The treaty also envisages new rules for EU organs and on how they function

2003
The Convent on the Future of Europe presents a Draft Treaty for a **European Constitution**

2004
The **Eastern enlargement** of the EU: On May 1, Cyprus, the Czech Republic, Estonia, Hungary, Latvia, Lithuania, Malta, Poland, Slovakia, and Slovenia join the EU. With more than 450 million inhabitants and economic output of EUR 10.7 trillion, the EU thus becomes the world's largest single market. On October 29, 2004 the Heads of State and Government sign the Constitutional Treaty for Europe

2005
On May 29 and June 1, the French and then the Dutch voted against the Draft Treaty for a Constitution, causing reflection on the EU's future. In October, the European Commission initiated accession negotiations with **Turkey** and **Croatia**

2007
Europe now has 27 member states. On January 1, **Bulgaria** and **Romania** accede to the European Union. In December, the heads of state and government sign the **EU Reform Treaty** destined to replace the failed EU Constitution

1990 2000 2010

21st century

Euro
The euro is the currency of the European Monetary Union and after the US dollar the second most important member of the international currency system. Together with the national central banks, the European Central Bank (ECB), headquartered in Frankfurt/Main, is responsible for monetary policy with regard to the euro. The euro is the official currency in 15 of the 27 EU member states. The euro was physically introduced in "Euroland", including Germany, on January 1, 2002, having served as a currency of deposit since the beginning of 1999.

integration – from the expansion of the Commission and the adoption of majority resolutions by the Council of the European Union (see p. 87) via the direct election of the European Parliament and the extension of common areas of responsibility through to major reforms in the form of the Treaties of Maastricht, Amsterdam and Nice. Thus, the treaty concluded in 2007 in Lisbon is a result of the Treaty of Rome and a consequence of the so-called "spill-over" of economic linkages into the political arena.

Without wanting to play down how important it is that Europe grow together politically, we should no doubt consider the economic dynamism triggered by integration and the attractiveness of the major market to be the key driving force prompting other European states to accede. This applies to the accession of Great Britain, Denmark and Ireland in the 1970s, that of Greece, Spain and Portugal in the 1980s, and of Austria, Sweden and Finland in the 1990s.

The European Union at a glance

Enlargement of the European Union
The European Union has successfully grown from 6 to 27 member states (2007). Croatia and Turkey are applicant countries, with whom accession negotiations have been initiated. The former Yugoslav Republic of Macedonia is an official access candidate, the other Western Balkan states potential candidates.

Likewise, it also applies to the magnetic appeal EU has had on the new democracies in the emerging market economies of Eastern Central Europe and South-East Europe. Just as was the case for the fledgling Federal Republic of Germany in the 1950s, the young democracies in the south and east of Europe rightly see accession to the EU as due recognition and assurance of the political achievements they have made in overcoming dictatorship and despotism. German European policy has unconditionally supported the ever-deeper integration process, its extension to the North, South and East as well as the establishment of the relevant institutions. The strength of German foreign policy has laid in ensuring Franco-German relations were firmly aligned to EU policy, on the one hand, and the close ties specifically to the smaller member states, on the other. Repeatedly, numerous hurdles to decisions have been overcome and key stages in the history of the EU have been successfully tackled as a result of Germany's efforts and its willingness to compromise.

Germany – a constructive EU member

Today the basic principles of German EU policy remain characterized by all-party consensus. The Germans desire a Europe that is capable of acting while remaining both democratic and transparent – and with a strengthened European Parliament. Like many other Europeans they reject the idea of a European super-state, preferring clearer delineation of areas of responsibility. Germany supports the pragmatic approach to integration taken with the EU Reform Treaty, but remains interested in further advances. The Germans know that they benefit economically and politically from Europe, the Common Market, the **euro** and from the EU's enlargement. The central position in the world's largest single market explains to a large extent Germany's prowess in the export league tables. In addition, today the economic relations with the country's neighbors in Eastern Central Europe can be fostered in line with the

European Parliament
The European Parliament is the parliamentary organ of the European communities. It is made up of 785 members (750 as of 2009 when the EU Reform Treaty is enacted), who are directly elected by the population of the 27 member states for five years. Each member state is allocated a certain number of seats depending on the size of its population. Germany, the largest member state of the EU, has 99 MEPs, and Malta, the smallest, 5 (as of 2009 Germany will have 96 seats, the smallest countries like Malta and Luxembourg have 6 seats). The members of the European Parliament represent a total of almost 500 million citizens. They form parliamentary groups independent of their own nationality. The Parliament has legislative, budgetary and monitoring powers, though no right of initiative in legislation. The Parliament sits in Strasbourg; plenary sessions and committee meetings also take place in Brussels.

The European Union facing major challenges: Federal Chancellor Angela Merkel and EU Commission President José Manuel Barroso

rules of integration. In each of these markets Germany is the largest foreign trading partner and usually German industry is the most important investor. At the same time Germany bears the consequences of European union in a particular way. It cannot protect its market in the east of the country from competition from EU partners. Germany carries a large part of the infrastructural burden of the new open borders because the major European transportation axes run through the country. In line with the country's gross domestic product the Germans provide some 20 percent of the EU budget.

The EU's future tasks

European energy and climate policy
In March 2007, during the German EU Council Presidency, the European Union laid new foundations for Europe's energy and climate protection policy. The heads of state and government resolved to enhance EU energy efficiency by 20 percent by 2020, to boost the proportion of renewable energy in the total consumed to 20 percent over the same time span, and to cut greenhouse gas emissions by at least 20 percent compared with the 1990 level (the "20/20/20 goals").

Since the development of European political cooperation one of Germany's wishes for the European Union is that the role the latter plays in world politics be strengthened. From a German point of view the security of EU members in the face of new types of threat is a joint task. In the global political arena the voice of Europe carries more weight than that of its individual member states. Like hardly any other state, Germany's foreign policy has made use of the EU as the basis for representation of its own interests and to promote these.

For many years now a steady majority in German public opinion has supported the idea that it is better to approach foreign and security policy questions as part of

Information on the Internet

www.auswaertiges-amt.de
Wide range of information from the Federal Foreign Office, also covering bilateral relations (Arabic, English, French, German, Spanish)

www.dgap.org
Website of the German Council on Foreign Relations (DGAP) - a network for foreign policy (English, German)

www.swp-berlin.org
Interesting scholarly Web site of the German think-tank Institute for International and Security Affairs (SWP) with articles and research findings on international politics and security policy (English, German)

www.eab-berlin.de
The European Academy Berlin sees itself as a European center of competence based in Germany's capital and offers countless outstanding conventions and seminars (English, German)

www.eu.int
The European Union's information portal covering all aspects of the community (23 languages)

an alliance. For this reason German European policy has championed the strengthening of the European ability to act, which involves strengthening the common foreign, security and defense policy. This is being implemented with the creation of the office of a "High Representative of Foreign and Security Policy" who will be responsible for the EU's foreign affairs.

The European Union has a strong interest in deeper partnership with the states of Central Asia. The German federal government therefore initiated an EU Central Asia strategy as part of its presidency of the EU Council in 2007. For the firs time, EU member states have defined their interests with regard to this important region and have set the key parameters for a future common policy.

Germany and its partners will face new challenges. The key coalitions and constellations of past decades will change, and a new balance of interests will test the ability of European politicians to forge compromises. In global economic terms there will be a shift, too – Europe's economy faces global competition. The EU's external borders interface with zones typified by low economic, political or social stability. The European Union must therefore field a trustworthy, active policy of development and partnership, not least for the countries on the Mediterranean rim.

Europe is not the place for small ideas. Without the European Union, welfare and security, those elementary services provided by the state, would no longer be possible. As such the policy of integration, the processes and the institutions are all part of Europe's political fabric and not mere frills.

Any major theme concerning European societies also addresses the EU's contribution to the issue, as there is hardly any issue that does not involve the European level. Germany, at the heart of political Europe, continues to view the European Union as the primary field of action for its international policy. ●

Council of the European Union
The Council, frequently referred to as the "Council of Ministers", is the EU's most important legislative committee. The Council and the European Parliament share legislative powers and responsibility for the EU budget. In addition the Council concludes international treaties negotiated by the Commission. Decisions can be made unanimously or with a qualified majority. In some policy areas, resolutions have to be unanimous. Otherwise, decisions are taken by qualified majority. The weighting of votes depends on the size of a country's population, but the smaller states have a disproportionately high number of votes. Germany holds 29 of the total of 345. The Chair (the Presidency of the Council) rotates every six months. On the institutional changes the EU Reform Treaty triggers as of 2009 see page 80.

Josef Janning
The political scientist and expert on European affairs is a member of the Board of the Bertelsmann Foundation.

6

The economy

Daimler, Siemens, Porsche, Lufthansa, SAP. In the international arena German companies have an excellent reputation. They represent "Made in Germany", known as a seal of quality the world over. They represent innovation, quality and cutting-edge technology. Yet the world's third largest economy does not consist solely of global players, but also of numerous world market leaders who are actually small and medium-sized enterprises, the powerhouse of the German economy. They all benefit from the sound economic conditions in the "land of ideas", not to mention the excellent qualifications of the workforce. Foreign investors also value this – and see it as a major point in Germany's favor in the age of the global economy.

The future of automobile production: On view in the VW "glass factory" in Dresden

Germany as an economic hub

By Thomas Straubhaar

GERMANY IS ONE OF THE MOST highly developed industrial nations in the world and, after the USA and Japan has the world's third largest national economy. With a population of 82.3 million Germany is also the largest and most important market in the European Union (EU). In 2007, Germany's gross domestic product (GDP) totaled EUR 2.42 trillion, which translates into per-capita GDP of EUR 29,455. This figure can be attributed primarily to foreign trade. With an **export** volume of EUR 969 billion or one third of GDP in 2007, Germany is the biggest exporter of goods worldwide, and as such is considered to be the "export world champion", more of a global player than almost any other country and more strongly linked to the global economy than many other countries. More than every fourth euro is earned from exported goods and services – and more than every fifth job depends on foreign trade. The most important economic centers in the country are the Ruhr region (formerly characterized by heavy industry, it is developing into a hub for high-tech and service providers), the Munich and Stuttgart conurbations (high-tech, automobiles), the Rhine/Neckar region (chemicals) Frankfurt/Main (finance), Cologne, Hamburg (port, Airbus construction, media) Berlin and Leipzig.

Most recently, the German economy has seen a robust upturn, growing 2.5 percent in 2007. The increase in corporate investments was especially pronounced at 8.4

Exports
Since 1991, the ratio of exports booked by the key exporting sectors has risen appreciably, testifying to German companies' strong competitive edge. Take the mechanical engineering sector, for example: There, between 1991 and 2006 the export ratio climbed from 52 percent to 77 percent, while in the chemicals industry it soared from 50 percent to over 70 percent. In the automobile industry the jump was from 43 percent to 72 percent, and in the electrical industry from 31 to 47 percent. The overall export ratio comes to 35 percent and Germany's share of total world trade stands at a nine percent.

Economic policy
In line with the federal system, structuring and coordinating economic and financial policy is the joint task of central government, the federal states and municipalities. They cooperate in various committees. Furthermore, the Federal Government seeks the advice of independent economists. Every January the Federal Government presents to the Bundestag and the Bundesrat the Annual Economic Report, which among other things describes the government's economic and financial goals for the year as well as the fundamentals of its planned economic and financial policy. One prerequisite for economic life in Germany being able to function is free competition, which is protected by the law against restrictions on competition.

percent. The economic growth, stimulated by factors both inside and outside Germany, sparked a reduction in the number of registered unemployed. In December 2007, the figure was 3.4 million, the lowest December level since 1992. A series of factors contributed to the favorable economic development and labor-market trend. **Economic policy** has improved the overall conditions and companies have sharpened their competitive edge. Thus, ancillary wage costs have been reduced, the labor market made more flexible and red tape slashed. Moreover, in 2008 corporation tax was reformed, further easing the strain on corporate Germany. Companies have at the same time optimized purchasing and cost structure, invested in innovative products, and are fitter to compete.

An attractive location for foreign investments

Germany is one of the most attractive countries world-wide for **international investors**, as is shown by recent polls of international managers and studied by renowned international consultants. In a study in 2007, auditors and consultant Ernst & Young examined the appeal of Europe as an economic region. They found that in the opinion of foreign

The economy in facts and figures

Germany ranks no. 3 in the world economy
USA, Japan and Germany are the three countries with the biggest national economies

2006 gross domestic product (in US$ billion)

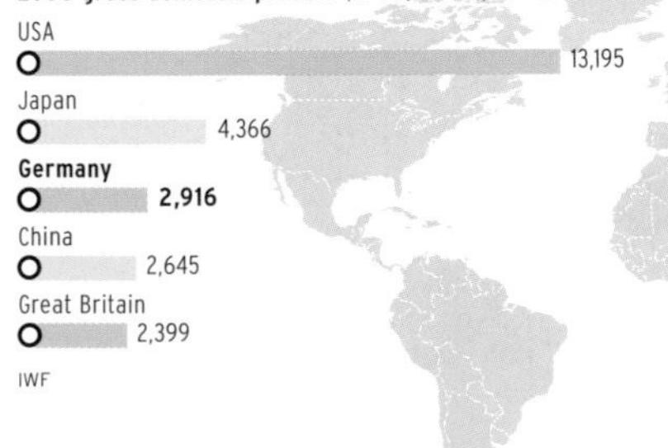

World export champions
Foreign trade as the powerhouse: The volume of German exports makes the country the world's no. 1

2006 Export volume (in US$ billion)

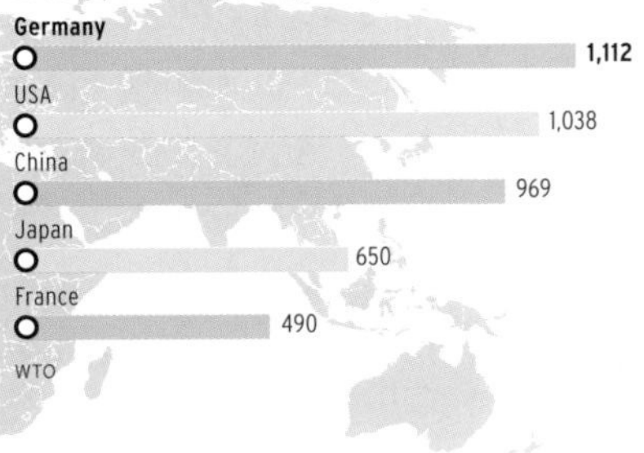

managers Germany is the leading country in Europe. On an international country comparison, Germany does especially well as regards R&D, skill levels and logistics. Moreover, it enjoys a central geographical position, offers strong infrastructure, legal certainty, and the right workforce. From 1996 to 2007, foreign direct investments (FDI) in Germany totaled US$ 473 billion, including major commitments by corporations such as General Electric and AMD – Germany thus places fifth in the FDI league tables.

The labor force's high level of qualifications is seen as an important plus point. Some 81 percent of those in employment have undergone formal training, and 20 percent hold a degree from a university or institute of higher education. The "dual system" for vocational training provides the bedrock here, combining on-the-job and college training, a policy which results in the well-known high standard of education.

Technology leader in many sectors

The country is likewise one of the leading nations as regards several of the technologies of the future that have exceptional growth rates. These include bio-technology,

International investors

Foreign firms value the strengths of the German market: Some 22,000 international companies operate here, including the world's top 500. Between 2007 and 2010, Spanish telco Telefónica O_2 Europe alone intends to invest EUR 3.5 bilion in expanding its fixed-line and mobile phone infrastructure in Germany. Among the major foreign investors are Californian chip producer Advanced Micro Devices (AMD), which in 2006-9 is investing some EUR 2 billion in expanding its chip factory in Dresden. In 2006, a total of US$ 42.9 billion was committed in capital by foreign private corporations in Germany. At the same time, the number of registered direct investment projects rose 57 percent and thus faster than in any other West European country.

Attractive location

International companies put Germany among the top 5 investment targets worldwide

Countries that are the most attractive investment targets worldwide (as a percentage of those polled)

Country	%
China	48
USA	33
India	26
Germany	**18**
Russia	12

Ernst & Young 2007

High degree of competitiveness

In terms of competitiveness, Germany is among the world leaders, placing no. 2 in a country comparison. Germany's enforcement of ownership laws and general law and order are considered to be particularly exemplary

Ranking of the world's most competitive countries (BCI Index)

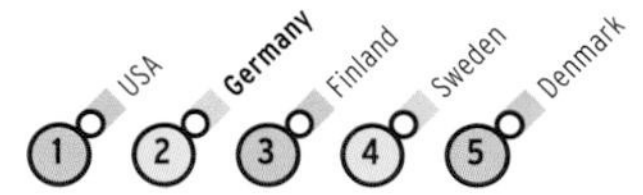

World Economic Forum 2007-2008

Germany – a place to do business I

Germany is one of the most important countries in which to do business: with excellent conditions for entrepreneurs, a modern infrastructure, and cutting-edge R&D

Independent collective bargaining
The collective wage bargaining partners – trade unions and employers and employers' associations – negotiate collective bargaining agreements. The state sets the general working conditions, though not how much workers are paid. This and the settlement of other questions – such as vacation and working hours – is left to collective bargaining. In some sectors, the state has mandated minimum wages to be set by collective wage bargaining

Wages
Labor market
Structure
Interests

Labor and employers

Trade unions and employers' associations
The largest association of trade unions is the Deutsche Gewerkschaftsbund (DGB), which has 6.4 million members. The DGB represents eight member trade unions, the largest is IG Metall. The employer associations are the unions' partners in wage negotiations. Their umbrella organization, the Bundesvereinigung der Deutschen Arbeitgeberverbände (BDA; Confederation of German Employers' Associations), represents some two million companies. Other business associations are: Deutscher Industrie- und Handelskammertag (DIHT; Association of German Chambers of Industry and Commerce), Bundesverband der Deutschen Industrie (BDI; Federation of German Industries)

The largest trade unions (in millions of members)

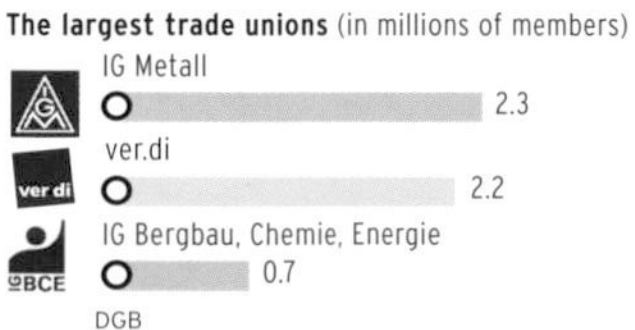

Labor market
About 40 million persons were gainfully employed in Germany at year-end 2007 – and thus more than ever before. At the same time, the number of unemployed fell to below 3.5 million. This prime trend was fostered by the strong economy, proactive labor market policies, lower ancillary wage costs, modest reforms to labor laws (in particular as regards protection against dismissal) and stronger investments in young people's qualifications

Employment structure
The vast majority of the approximate 40 million employed and self-employed in Germany works in the service sector and in manufacturing

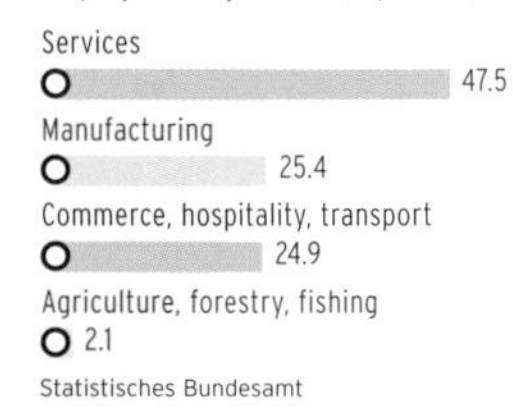

Mobility and logistics

Germany boasts a highly-developed infrastructure. A closely knit network of more than 230,000 kilometers of roads, of which some 12,000 kilometers are interstates, as well as around 36,000 kilometers of rail tracks, make Germany a hub for European long-distance freight. Frankfurt airport, the largest in continental Europe, and a close network of regional airports, guarantee international access

Taxes and welfare contributions

Germany has long since ceased to be a country with high taxation. Compared with other countries it has below-average taxation and welfare contribution levels. As regards income and earnings, in terms of economic output German taxation levels are among the lowest of European industrial countries

Income and earnings tax
(as a ratio of economic performance in 2005)

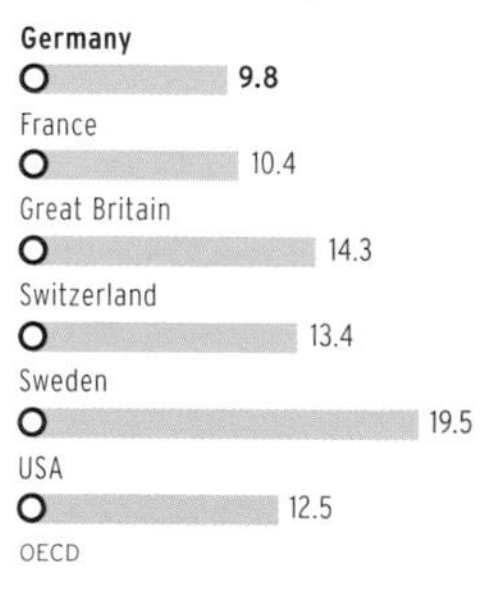

Qualifications

"Made in Germany" is a quality seal that attests to the fact that Germany is the market leader in several industrial and commercial sectors. High levels of education, high productivity levels and the close networking of industry, science and research make this possible

Share of the population with high level of schooling (2005, in percent)

Country	Percent
Germany	83
Great Britain	67
France	66
Italy	50
Spain	49

OECD

R&D

From the point of view of foreign companies Germany is the most attractive European country for R&D. In 2007, a poll of international companies conducted by Ernst & Young revealed that Germany was the favorite in terms of R&D facilities

Attractive in terms of R&D in Europe
(as a percentage of those polled)

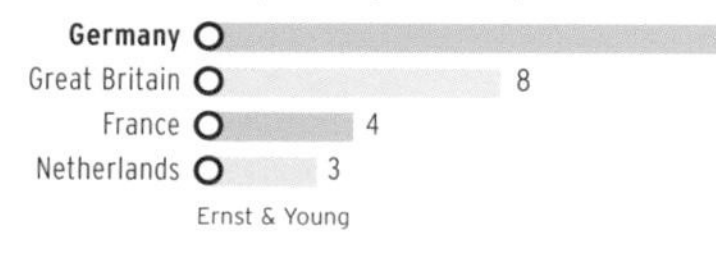

Bright outlook: Germany offers rosy prospects for high-tech companies

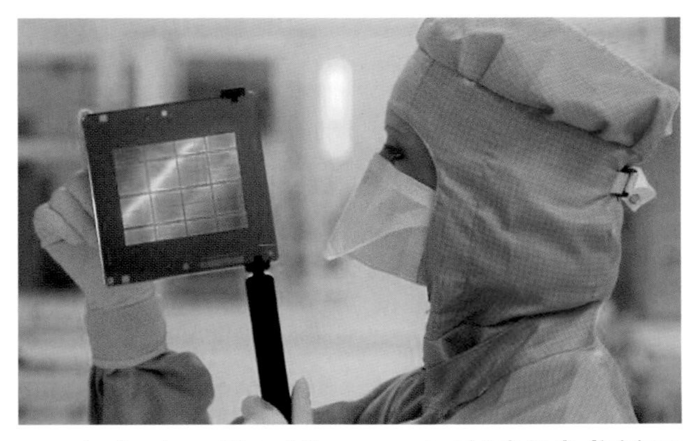

Information and communications technology (ICT)
Germany is a leading country in ICT, with computer technology in place in 84 percent of companies and 71 percent of private homes. Germany is well above the European average, with 76 percent of the population using a PC and 69 percent surfing the Internet. Today, Germany is also the biggest mobile phone and online market in all of Europe. 94 percent of households have a land line, and 81 percent at least one mobile phone, too. About 475,000 persons work in the German ICT sector, with Germany accounting for six percent of the global ICT market.

nano-technology, IT and the numerous high-tech divisions in individual sectors (aviation and aerospace, electrical engineering, logistics). Companies specializing in environmental technology (wind energy, photovoltaic power and biomass generation) have emerged as front runners. The German environmental technology branch (wind energy, photovoltaics, bio-mass) is also well established in international markets, with manufacturers of wind energy plants boasting a 50% share of the market (see chapter 7). Today, **Information and communications technology** follows car-making and electronics/electrical engineering as the third largest sector of the economy. As regards bio- and genetic engineering, Germany is second to the United States worldwide and already has a knowledge edge in many fields of nanotechnology.

However, it is not only major corporations such as Siemens, Volkswagen or BASF that lay the foundations for the German economy to be competitive in the international arena, but also tens of thousands of small and medium-sized enterprises (so-called SMEs, with up to 500 employees) in the manufacturing sector, in particular mechanical engineering, the components industry as well as nano- and bio-technology, which frequently form **clusters**. With over 20 million employees these SMEs together easily constitute Germany's biggest employer. They also provide the lion's share of traineeships for young people.

The key industrial sectors

Industry accounts for 87 percent (2006) of total exports and is thus the engine driving foreign trade. The key industrial sectors are car-making, electronics, mechanical engineering and chemicals. Some 2.88 million people are employed in these four sectors alone, which book sales of EUR 767 billion. As is the case in all western industrial nations, for several years now German industry has been in the midst of structural transformation. Some traditional industries (steel, textiles) have in partly shrunk considerably in recent years, with target markets now elsewhere and strong pressure from low-wage countries, or, as in the case of the pharmaceuticals industry, through M&As have come under foreign ownership. Yet, industry continues to be the backbone of the German economy and in comparison with other industrial countries such as Great Britain and the USA is extremely broad-based – eight million people work in industrial companies.

Cluster
A critical mass of companies located in close proximity to one another is referred to as a cluster. Clusters are networks of manufacturers, suppliers and research institutes created along one and the same value-added chain. With regard to future technologies in particular clusters are considered to be the powerhouses driving innovation. Examples of successful clusters are the automobile industry in Baden-Württemberg, the concentration of medical technology firms in Tuttlingen, the chip belt girdling Dresden and the biotechnology cluster in the Berlin/Brandenburg region, which considers itself to be the leading life-science hub in Germany.

SMEs, the backbone of the economy

The German economy is characterized first and foremost by around 3.6 million small and medium-sized enterprises as well as the self-employed and the independent professions. Some 99.7 percent of all companies are small and medium-sized enterprises. These are firms with annual sales of below EUR 50 million and a payroll of less than 500. Around 70 percent of all those in employment work in this type of SME.

A look at the various economic sectors reveals that 48.9 percent of all SMEs operate as service providers, 31.4 percent in manufacturing, and around 19.7 percent in commerce. Most SMEs are managed by the owners themselves, meaning that the majority shareholder and management of the company are frequently one and the same. Companies are often handed down from one generation to the next. Around 95 percent of German companies are family-owned and almost every third company now has a woman at its head. In 2006 alone, 471,200 new companies started up (compared with 430,700 cases of bankruptcy).

In support of SMEs the Federal government enacted a bill creating more scope for SMEs, easing the red tape they face and simplifying procedures overall. The strengths of SMEs include the swift realization of marketable products, an international focus, a high degree of specialization and the ability to successfully claim niche positions in the market.

Innovations
Vehicle construction has a significant lead in terms of sales levels booked with new products. It alone accounts for almost 28 percent of all sales of innovative products in the German economy. New products account for a full 56 percent of overall sales in the vehicle construction sector.

Car-making: The strongest sector

Car-making is one of the most important sectors in German industry, accounting as it does for every seventh employee and 17 percent of all exports. Thanks to its six renowned manufacturers VW, Audi, BMW, Daimler, Porsche and Opel (General Motors), Germany takes its place alongside Japan and the USA as one of the top three automobile manufacturers in the world. Each year some six million new cars roll off German lines, and German marques produce an additional 5.5 million vehicles outside the country.

In particular, customers set great store by the technical **innovations** which vehicles "made in Germany" feature. All the car makers are now busy developing eco-friendly engines such as a new generation of diesel motors, hybrid drives and further electrification of power transmissions.

Reforms for economy and society

The Federal government's express aims are to buttress the upturn, continue public budget consolidation and unleash additional intrinsic economic growth drivers. One of the tools to achieve this is a future fund of EUR 25 billion that through 2009 will enable investments in key areas such as traffic infrastructure, education, research, technology, as well as family promotion. Investment incentives are to be strengthened and Germany's appeal on an international fiscal comparison are to be boosted by reducing bureaucracy, clearly cutting tax rates for companies, and simplifying company succession arrangements as regards inheritance tax. The other major challenges of the day are climate protection, energy provision, health, security, and mobility. The Federal government seeks to tackle them with an overarching "high-tech strategy": The worlds of science, business and politics are to join forces to boost Germany's technological prowess. In 17 "fields of the future", such as bio-, nano- and eco-tech, or ICT, alliances between science and industry are set to tap new markets or expand existing ones. To this end, joint projects between the two communities will be promoted, with research findings being implemented faster and tests for their economic feasibility involving less red tape. In pursuit of this goal, the Federal government is making some EUR 15 billion available through 2009.

Electronics and chemicals: innovative and international

Companies in the electronics and electrical engineering sector are active in a whole host of areas, from electronic appliances via measuring technology to chip production. The scale of research outlays here reflects the pronounced focus on innovation. The figure came to EUR 9.4 billion in 2006, with Siemens registering almost 1,500 international patents that year, placing third world-wide. The chemicals industry is likewise a champion, and primarily makes intermediate products. Indeed, Ludwigshafen-based BASF is the world's largest chemicals corporation.

Modern production facilities for top-quality products: Flexibility is prioritized in the BMW works in Leipzig. In the factory the machines run for up to 140 hours a week

Service providers: The single largest sector

Almost 28 million people work in the flourishing service sector in the broadest sense – around 12 million of them are

Innovation for the future

German companies and researchers are busy trail-blazing in all key industries of tomorrow. Nanotechnology is considered to be "the" technology of the future. It comprises research and construction in extremely small structures – a nanometer is a millionth of a millimeter. Nanotechnology is working on the fundamentals for ever smaller data memories delivering ever greater capacity, for example for photovoltaic windows, for tools that can be used to produce ultra-light engines and body parts in the automobile industry, and for artificial limbs that thanks to organic nano-scale outer surfaces are more compatible with the human body. At a rough estimate, the USA and Europe have the same amount of companies engaged in nanotechnology. And of the firms in Europe around 50 percent come from Germany.

There are also more than 600 German companies operating successfully in the highly diverse sector of biotechnology. Alongside other projects they address the development of new methods and processes in biomedicine technology, biomaterial research, the food industry, pest control and innovations in the pharmaceutical and chemical industries.

Germany is also a leader in environmental technology, accounting for some 19 percent of world trade with its exports of goods for environmental protection, and leads the way in the registration of eco-patents with the European Patents Office. In order to build on these achievements, the federal government is investing EUR 6 billion through 2010 in R&D in the "technologies of tomorrow".

Germany – a place to do business II

With 160 international trade fairs, Germany is an important "marketplace" for goods of all descriptions

The largest German industrial corporations

Who are the "biggest" in the country? With sales totaling over EUR 151 billion in 2006, DaimlerChrysler has a clear lead over its competitor Volkswagen (at the end of 2007 Daimler shed Chrysler). In terms of payroll Siemens leads the way. With 475,000 members of staff, the company is the largest private employer in Germany

The largest German industrial companies in terms of sales in 2006 (in EUR million)

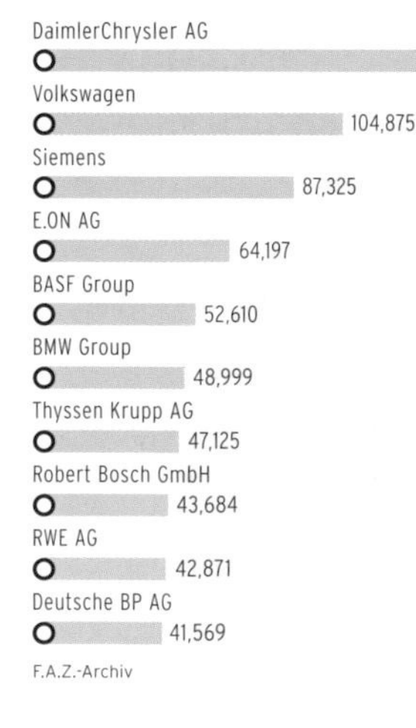

The stock exchange and banks

Frankfurt/Main is the leading banking center in continental Europe, with over 100 of the Top 500 bank institutes based there. It is the seat of the European Central Bank (ECB), the German Bundesbank and the Frankfurt stock exchange. Major German corporations are traded on the Deutscher Aktien Index (DAX). Germany's largest bank is Deutsche Bank, with a balance sheet total of EUR 1,126 billion and about 69,000 employees

Top brands from Germany

Mercedes, BMW, SAP, Siemens, Volkswagen, Adidas-Salomon and Porsche are among the highest valued brands worldwide. In the international league table of most valuable brands of 2007 (Business Week) German companies are listed ten times, making them the second largest group after the USA in the Top 100 global trade marks

The large service providers

Deutsche Telekom AG (EUR 61.3 billion) and Deutsche Post AG (EUR 60.5 billion) clearly lead the way in terms of service providers with the highest sales. With 520,000 employees, Deutsche Post is also the largest employer in this business sector. Deutsche Bahn, the travel company TUI from Hanover, the media Group Bertelsmann and Deutsche Lufthansa, with sales totaling EUR 20 billion and some 95,000 employees, follow

The largest service providers in terms of sales (in EUR million in 2006)

Deutsche Telekom AG	61,347
Deutsche Post AG	60,545
Deutsche Bahn AG	30,053
TUI AG	20,515
Deutsche Lufthansa	19,849

F.A.Z.-Archiv

CeBIT

Digital worlds: With over 6,000 exhibitors (50 percent of them from abroad) and 280,000 square meters of exhibition space, CeBIT, which has been held for many years every spring in Hanover, is considered to be the world's leading IT trade fair

www.cebit.de

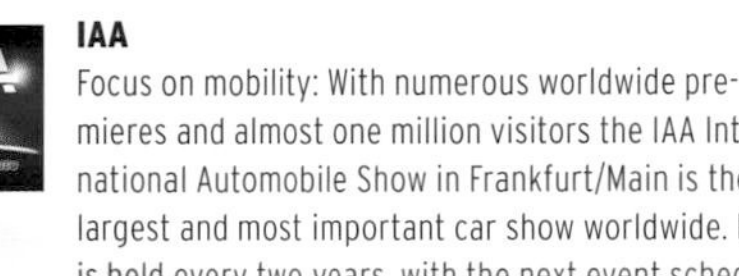

IAA

Focus on mobility: With numerous worldwide premieres and almost one million visitors the IAA International Automobile Show in Frankfurt/Main is the largest and most important car show worldwide. It is held every two years, with the next event scheduled for 2009

www.iaa.de

Hanover Trade Fair

The Hanover Trade Fair is the showcase for industry. More than 6,400 exhibitors from around 70 countries regularly take part in the Hanover Trade Fair. Every April they make the fair one of the world's most important events for technology, featuring everything from process automation and pipeline technologies to micro-system technology

www.hannovermesse.de

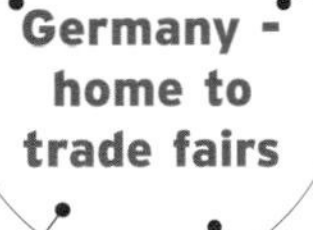

IFA

Representatives of the entertainment and communications technology sector meet each year at the IFA International Broadcasting Fair in Berlin. With more than 1,200 exhibitors and over 220,000 visitors, the IFA showcases innovative entertainment technology

www.ifa-berlin.de

ITB

Travel fever: The International Tourism Exchange Berlin is the name of the international tourism industry's leading specialist trade fair. Every year more than 10,000 exhibitors attend (80 percent of them from abroad) not to mention more than 175,000 visitors

www.itb-berlin.de

AUMA

AUMA, the German business community's exhibitions and trade-fair committee, is the leading association in the German trade-fair segment. Its key task is to strengthen German trade fairs at home and abroad. AUMA also coordinates German business' trade fairs outside the country, among others on behalf of the approx. 230 export platforms supported by the Federal government each year. The organizers under the AUMA umbrella also arrange over 200 annual trade fairs of their own in key foreign growth regions

www.auma-messen.de

32,500 R&D staff in more than 30 countries: Siemens is seen as the key innovation driver in Germany

active in private and public service providers, almost ten million in commerce, the hospitality industry and transportation, with six million working in financing, leasing and corporate services. The sector is another characterized by a large number of SMEs, which account for a good 40 percent of the companies operating in it.

Of total gross value added of EUR 2,094 billion in the country, private and public service providers already contribute EUR 468 billion (2006) and companies involved in financing, leasing and corporate services generate an additional EUR 618 billion. A key pillar of the services sector: banking and insurance companies. They are concentrated in Frankfurt/Main, which is home to both the European Central Bank (ECB), the guardian of the euro, the German Bundesbank, and Deutsche Börse. Another sector is gradually emerging as a big hitter: culture. Also known as the creative industries, the sector includes music, literature, art, film and the performing arts, not to mention radio/TV, the press, advertising, design and software. Although there is no statistical base yet available, the creative industries have emerged as a stable economic factor in many regions, such as Berlin.

R&D as a driving force

As Germany is a so-called high-wage country, it is particularly important for German companies to be one step ahead of their competitors in terms of quality. To this end Germany currently commits around 2.5 percent of its GDP to research and development (R&D), considerably more than the EU average of around 1.8 percent (2006). The Federal Government plans to increase spending on R&D to three percent of the country's GDP by the year 2010. Moreover, Germany is also a leader as regards company-financed R&D, where the figure comes to some USD 45 billion.

The spirit of invention continues to thrive: In 2006, investors and companies from Germany accounted for over 11.7 percent of patents worldwide – putting the country at no. 3 in the international rankings.

East Germany is catching up

Productivity
GDP per employed,
in respective prices

	Old states	New states
1991	45,235	20,150
2006	61,417	48,277

Fixed asset investments
per citizen in euro

	Old states	New states
1991	4,800	3,300
2006	4,800	4,000

Bundesministerium für Wirtschaft und Technologie

Successful: Germany in the global economy

Given its high level of exports, Germany is interested in open markets. The most important trading partners are

Aufbau Ost – economic reconstruction in the East

Following reunification of the two German states in 1990 Germany faced a challenge that was unique in history. The aim was to bring living conditions in both East and West closer together. As almost the entire East German industry was outdated, enormous efforts were called for to modernize it. Since reunification around EUR 80 billion or around three percent of the GDP of the entire country have been transferred annually. However, the convergence process is proving to be more long-term than originally foreseen. In the meantime, a small but efficient industrial sector has developed in various high-tech centers, so-called "beacon regions" in the five new federal states. These include the regions around Dresden, Jena, Leipzig, Leuna, and Berlin/Brandenburg. The manufacturing industry has established itself as the new powerhouse driving growth. Production rates continue to be high. As unit labor costs are lower than the West German average and almost only cutting-edge technology is used, standards in this particular sector are almost on a par with those in the old federal states. In 2005, per capita disposable income was around EUR 14,400 (EUR 18,500 in the old federal states) and has doubled since 1991. Nonetheless, fighting unemployment in East Germany is still a challenge. Totaling EUR 156 billion, Solidarity Pact II, which came into force in 2005, provides the financial basis for the advancement and special promotion of federal states in East Germany until 2019.

Social market economy
The Basic Law of the Federal Republic of Germany does not call for any particular economic order. Yet it is firmly anchored in the principle of the welfare state and therefore excludes a purely free market economy. Since the founding of the Federal Republic of Germany in 1949 the country's economic policy has been hinged on the notion of the social market economy. This concept is an attempt to find a happy medium between a pure market economy and socialism. The social market economy was developed and implemented by Ludwig Erhard, the first Minister of Economics and later German Chancellor. The fundamental idea is based on the principle of freedom of a market economy, supplemented by socio-political methods for keeping a due balance in society. On the one hand, the system is designed to enable market forces in principle to develop freely. On the other, the state guarantees a welfare network that protects its citizens from risks.

France, the USA and Great Britain. In 2006, goods and services worth EUR 85 billion were exported to France, EUR 78 billion to the USA and EUR 65 billion to Great Britain.

In addition to trade with the original European Union member states, since the EU's expansion eastwards (2004 and 2007) there has been a pronounced increase in trade with the east European EU member states. In total, a good ten percent of all exports go to these countries. The importance of trade and economic relations with emerging nations in Asia such as China and India is growing continually. While German exports to these regions came to EUR 33 billion in 1993, the figure has now more than tripled to EUR 104 billion (2006). The number of German companies in Asia rose over the same period from 1,800 to 3,500, with direct investments more than quadrupling over the same period.

Germany is a **social market economy**, in other words: The state guarantees the free play of entrepreneurial forces, while at the same time endeavoring to maintain the social balance. This concept is another strong reason why Germany enjoys such a high degree of social harmony, something reflected in the fact that labor disputes are so rare here. On average between 1996 and 2005 the work force went on strike for on just 2.4 days per 1,000 employees and thus less than even Switzerland, which saw 3.1 days of strikes. The social partnership of trade

Information on the Internet

www.invest-in-germany.de
The Web site of the Invest in Germany GmbH federal agency provides legal, business and sector data, coordinates location processes with local partners, and helps companies contact the right people (in six languages)

www.bmwi.de
The Federal Ministry of Economics and Technology Web site provides data from quality management to e-commerce, infos and links (English, French, German)

www.ahk.de
The Web site of the German Chambers of Commerce Abroad provides information for German companies planning to invest abroad (English, German)

www.german-business-portal.info
The BMWI services and information focus on the international community (English)

www.ixpos.de
Ixpos presents a overview of services promoting German foreign trade (German)

Operating worldwide: German companies are intimately familiar with the global market and are well positioned in it

unions and employer associations is enshrined in the institutionalized settlement of conflicts as outlined in the collective labor law. The Basic Law guarantees the social partners independence in negotiating wages, and they accordingly have the right themselves to select the working conditions. ●

Thomas Straubhaar
The Swiss professor of economics is Director of the Hamburg Institute of International Economics (HWWI) and one of the most prominent economists in Germany.

7

Environment, climate, energy

Changes in the atmosphere and climate system are among the greatest environmental and political challenges of the 21st century. Climate change, which has largely been caused by human activity, is *the* global challenge. For many years now, Germany has been making efforts to avoid greenhouse gas emissions by way of anticipatory national climate change policies and by promoting renewable energy sources and energy efficiency. In the international arena, Germany is a forerunner in climate and energy policies and seeks to achieve ambitious emission-reduction goals.

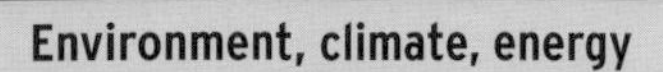

Renewable energy is a must if we want to save the climate. It will play an important role in the energy mix of the future

Paths to a modern and sustainable climate and energy policy

By Joachim Wille

THE PROTECTION OF THE ENVIRONMENT AND CLIMATE is among the global challenges of the 21st century and is accorded a prime status in German politics, media and civil society. Germany is internationally considered one of the forerunners in climate protection and a pioneer in developing renewable energies. And the government assumes an active role in environmental protection, climate-friendly development strategies and energy partnerships at the global level, too. The Secretariat which supports the operation of the United Nations **Framework Convention on Climate Change** is headquartered in Bonn. Since 1990, Germany has reduced its greenhouse gas emissions by almost 20 percent and thus is already very close to its obligations outlined in the Kyoto Protocol of a 21-percent reduction by 2012. Germany places second in the global Climate Change Performance Index 2008, compiled by independent environmental protection organization "Germanwatch". For many years now, Germany has been following a course which unites climate and environmental protection in terms of sustainable management. The key: a dual strategy to increase energy and resource efficiency and to develop renewable energies and raw materials. This promotes the development of innovative energy technologies both on the supply side, in power stations and renewable energy plants, and on the demand side, where energy is used, for example, in household appliances, cars and buildings.

Nature conservation ("the conservation and protection of the natural foundations of life") has been enshrined

Framework Convention on Climate Change
In global terms, the United Nations Framework Convention on Climate Change (UNFCCC) and the Kyoto Protocol linked to it are the only internationally legally binding regulations on climate protection. The 189 signatory countries at present meet annually at the UN Climate Change Conference. The best-known of these conferences took place in 1997 in Kyoto, Japan and resulted in the Kyoto Protocol. It fixed the reduction of greenhouse gas emissions of all developed countries at a certain level. At present, the so-called post-Kyoto process is starting, and will include negotiations on climate change policy from 2012 until 2020.

"World champion in wind energy" Germany: No other country produces a similar amount of electricity from wind power

Greenhouse gas emission
Roughly two thirds of global warming caused by humans (anthropogenic) can be attributed to carbon dioxide (CO_2) emissions. The gas is produced when the fossil fuels gas, oil and coal are burned. They all contain carbon (C) which combines with atmospheric oxygen (O_2) to form CO_2. According to studies by the International Energy Agency (IEA), energy-related anthropogenic activity releases over 26 billion tons of CO_2 into the atmosphere every year. In addition to carbon dioxide, other greenhouse gases regulated by the Kyoto Protocol are nitrous oxide, methane, fluorocarbons and sulfur hexafluoride.

as a state objective in Article 20a of the Basic Law since 1994. Intact natural systems, pure air and clean waterways are preconditions for a high quality of life and of the environment in Germany. Environmental indicators are pointing in a positive direction as regards the prevention of air and water pollution, because many emissions have been considerably reduced in recent years. **Greenhouse gas emissions** from road traffic have been decreasing since 1999, despite a significant increase in traffic; indeed, in 2005, for example, they were at the same level as in 1990. Outfitting motor vehicles with catalytic converters is, along with other measures, partly responsible for a roughly 50 percent reduction in nitrous oxide emissions. Sulfur dioxide emissions from coal and lignite power stations were able to be slashed by 90 percent owing to the mandatory flue gas desulfurization process. In recent years, the daily per capita rate of drinking water consumption has also decreased from 144 liters to 126 liters, the second lowest rate of all industrialized countries.

Fossil fuels still make up the backbone of the energy mix both in private households and for traffic and industry. With a 36-percent share, petroleum is the most important primary energy source, followed by natural gas, coal, nuclear fuel and lignite. Nuclear power, which is only used in the electricity sector, where it accounts for around 25 percent of total generation, is being gradually phased out, in accordance with a "nuclear consensus" concluded in 2000 between the federal government and electricity providers.

Trailblazing and efficient: Renewable energy

Against the background of the consequences of climate change, which science has described in vivid detail and which include increases in temperature, floods, droughts, accelerated melting of the polar icecaps and species extinction, as well as the constantly increasing global consumption of fossil fuels, renewable, climate-friendly alternatives are becoming increasingly more significant. The availability of wind, water, sun, biomass and geothermal energy is unlimited and they release no emissions which are damaging to the climate. Renewable energies now make up 8.4 percent (2007) of all German energy consumption and as much as 14 percent of electricity consumption. Experts project a systematic increase in the latter to a level of 25 to 30 percent by 2020. With almost 30 percent of global wind energy output, Germany is considered the "world champion in wind energy". Photovoltaic technology, which is used to turn the sun's rays into electricity, is likewise demonstrating a swift rate of development and innovation. And biomass fuels such as biodiesel and bioethanol are being mixed with petrol in increasing quantities.

Successful and exemplary: State subsidies policy

The subsidies policy implemented as far back as the beginning of the 1990s makes the use of renewable energy attractive and economical. The **Renewable Energy Sources Act**

Renewable Energy Sources Act
The Renewable Energy Sources Act (EEG) is intended to advance the development of energy supply facilities driven by self-renewing sources. The goal is to increase the percentage of renewable energies in electricity consumption from the current level of 14.3 percent to a target corridor of 25-30 percent in 2020. The EEG guarantees producers compensation at fixed rates. The law, which came into force in 2000, is one of a series of measures aimed at reducing dependence on fossil fuels and energy imports from outside the EU. 47 other states have adopted the basic features of the German EEG.

Nature conservation and biological diversity

There are around 45,000 native animal species and over 30,000 native species of land plants, mosses, fungi, lichens and algae in Germany. Nature conservation is a state goal in the Federal Republic and is entrenched in Article 20a of the Basic Law. There are thousands of designated nature conservation areas in Germany, as well as 14 national parks and an equal number of biosphere reserves. In addition, Germany is party to nine global, 11 regional and almost 30 international agreements which strive to conserve the environment. In Johannesburg the heads of state and government pledged to significantly reduce the current rate of loss of biological diversity by 2010. At the Göteborg Summit in 2001, the EU was even more ambitious resolving to stop biodiversity loss by 2010. The 9th Conference of the Parties to the Convention on Biological Diversity took place in Bonn in 2008.
Nonetheless, there is still much work to be done. Around 40 percent of animal species and 20 percent of plant species in Germany are deemed endangered. The reasons include the destruction and disintegration of their habitats by housing estates and road construction, the intensification of agriculture and forestry, pollution and excess fertilization. The percentage of organically managed areas has continually increased in Germany from 4.9 percent in 2006 and is projected to rise to 20 percent in the medium term. Consumers are also recognizing the value of organic products; in late 2007, a total of 42,825 notifications of organic products had been sent to the Bio-Siegel information center for official recognition.

Integrated Energy and Climate Program
The Federal government intends to reduce German greenhouse gas emissions by 40 percent by 2020 with an Integrated Energy and Climate Program. The program encompasses measures in 29 fields ranging from the promotion of co-generation (facilities which generate electricity and heat at the same time) and of renewable energy to the continued development of carbon capture and storage technology (CCS), i.e., the separation and storage of carbon dioxide which accumulates in the power-generation process. The Federal government is pursuing three central goals with the Climate Program, namely, improving safe energy supplies, cost-effectiveness and lowering environmental impact.

(EEG), a market incentive program to foster the use of renewable energy, is considered the driver of the boom in climate-friendly energy sources and many countries have adopted its basic features. The increased use of renewable energy and a more efficient use of energy also form the core of the **Integrated Energy and Climate Program**, which the German government adopted in late 2007. The objective of the climate program, which has several stages, is to further separate economic development from emissions, to significantly increase energy efficiency and to guarantee safe energy supplies. This self-set climate package is intended to ensure that CO_2 emissions are reduced by 40 percent of the 1990 level by 2020. Germany has thus put itself at the top of the international leader board; no other comparable industrialized country has a similarly ambitious and concrete program.

Innovative and good for exports: Green technologies

These measures not only serve to protect the environment, but also to promote the development of an innovative future industry, which is a real job creator, is highly internationally competitive and increasingly active in foreign

Energy and the environment in facts and figures

Greenhouse gas reduction: Europe is making headway
The EU still has to reduce greenhouse gas emissions by approximately 11.5 percent in order to achieve a 20 percent reduction on the 1990 level. On comparison, the EU is doing well

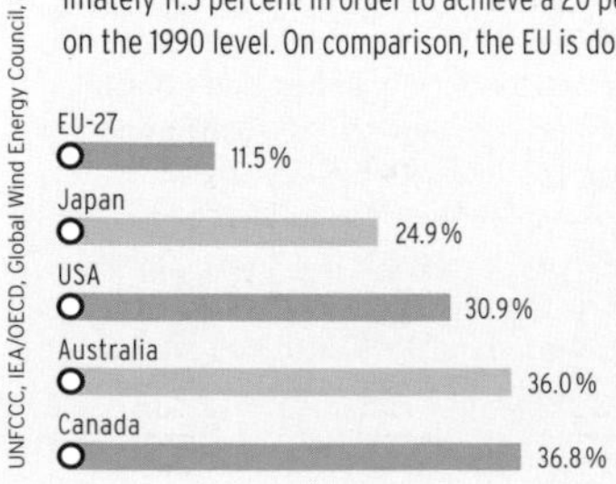

Energy intensity: Efficient Germany
With an energy input of 98 kilograms of oil equivalent, Germany achieves an industrial added value of USD 1,000

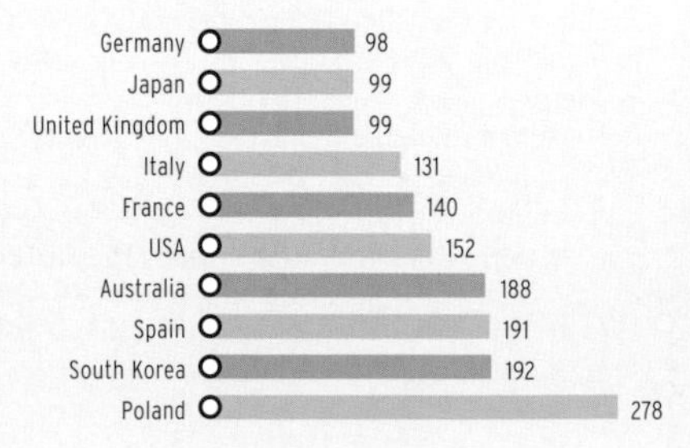

UNFCCC, IEA/OECD, Global Wind Energy Council, BEE

markets. Now, every third solar cell and almost every second wind turbine come from Germany. In 2007, more than 250,000 people were working in the renewable energies industry. In addition there are around one million more jobs in environmental technology, which includes water purification, filter technology, recycling and renaturalization. Another job driver are companies, too, which in times of rising energy prices are focusing on energy efficiency technologies (power stations with higher levels of efficiency, combined generation of electricity and heat, energy efficient construction, energetic building renovation, energy-saving cars). According to information from the International Energy Agency (IEA), Germany is already in the top group of countries which demonstrate a substantial economic performance with relatively low energy use. A study by the renowned corporate consultants Roland Berger states that by 2020, the environmental industry may provide more jobs than the machine construction and automobile industries, which still employ a great many people today. Moreover, two thirds of the population are convinced that consistent environmental policies have a positive influence on the competitiveness of the economy.

Environmental technologies as job drivers: The eco-industry is projected to be one of the most important job sectors in only 15 years time

"World champion in wind energy": Germany

With an installed capacity of 20,622 megawatts, Germany is the world's largest market for wind energy

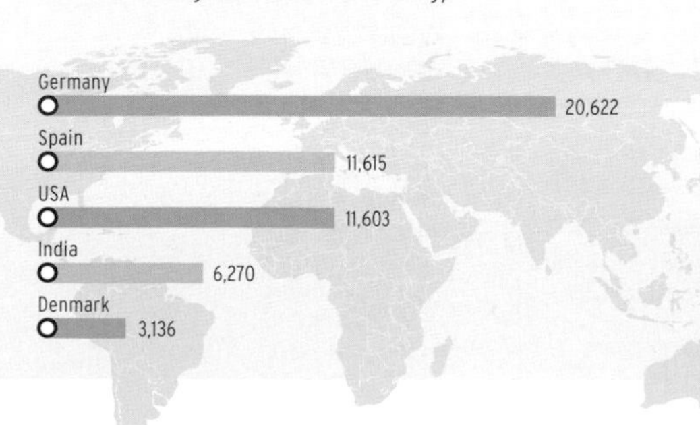

Carbon dioxide: emissions avoided

In 2007, renewable energies reduced CO_2 emissions in Germany by 115.3 million tons - and it is set to increase

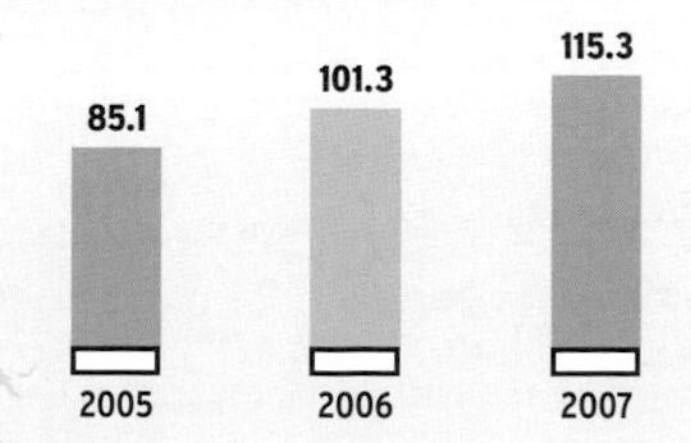

Necessary: International cooperation on the climate

EU climate goals
In early 2008, the EU Commission presented its proposals for realizing the EU climate and energy package in national quotas. Germany will make an above-average contribution to cutting greenhouse gas emissions in Europe. In the sectors traffic, buildings and agriculture, a reduction of 14 percent in carbon dioxide emissions by 2020 is projected for the Federal Republic. The percentage of renewable energy in Germany's entire energy consumption is also projected to double, from 9 percent (2007) to 18 percent, by 2020.

Climate change, the hole in the ozone layer and the pollution of the seas do not stop at national borders, therefore the protection of the environment and climate is an important task for the international community of nations.

Thus the German EU and G8 presidencies in 2007 made **climate protection objectives** and energy policy two of their main goals. The European Council, with its challenging resolutions in March 2007 to reduce greenhouse gas emissions, and the declaration of the G8 Summit in Heiligendamm, Germany, where heads of state and government pledged "to seriously test" the objective to halve greenhouse gas emissions by 2050, were important steps towards a global answer to climate change. Accordingly, the EU intends to reduce emissions of greenhouse gas such as CO_2 by at least 20 percent compared to the 1990 level by 2020, or by 30 percent if other industrial nations commit to similar reductions. It also intends to increase the share of renewable energy to 20 percent and lower energy consumption by 20 percent by means of improved energy efficiency. Emissions trading with CO_2 pollution rights for industry and electricity providers is to be an efficient and precise instrument in achieving these objectives. The EU has been testing this measure since 2005, which covers around half of greenhouse gas emissions.

The German Federal Government's seeks to actively involve economically advanced emerging nations such

The topic on the Internet

www.bmu.de
The Federal Ministry for the Environment, Nature Conservation and Nuclear Safety (BMU) presents on its Web site the most important political fields of action (German, English)

www.umweltbundesamt.de
The Federal Environment Agency (UBA) is Germany's central authority on the environment regarding virtually all issues of environmental protection. The UBA Web site provides information on relevant environmental topics (German, English)

www.pik-potsdam.de
The Potsdam Institute for Climate Impact Research (PIK) investigates climate change in all its complexity. The PIK is part of the Leibniz Association and is supported equally by the Federal Republic of Germany and the State of Brandenburg (German, English)

unfccc.int
Website of the United Nations Framework Convention on Climate Change with relevant information (English, French, Spanish)

as China, India, South Africa, Brazil and Mexico in protecting the climate too. This is a decisive point, for according to forecasts by the **United Nations Climate Council IPCC**, global CO_2 emissions must be halved by 2050 if global warming is to remain manageable in this century. As such, it is necessary to prevent the average global temperature rising by more than 2°C. This goal will not be achieved by the Kyoto Protocol, which came into force in February 2005 and in which only the industrialized countries were bound to a CO_2 reduction of 5.2 percent by 2012. As part of the "post-Kyoto process," the German government is calling for a successor protocol with more demanding obligations to reduce emissions. It would expire in 2020 and achieve a reversal of the trend on a global scale.

The Climate Change Conference in Bali in late 2007 laid the foundations for this. After complex negotiations, over 180 countries agreed to a negotiation framework for a regime that will succeed Kyoto. The developed nations want to significantly increase their efforts and, for the first time, developing and emerging nations also want to take measures to control their CO_2 emissions. In addition, in 2008 an adjustment fund was started, designed to help developing countries combat the consequences of global warming. The adjustment fund, managed by the World Bank and the Global Environment Fund (GEF), is projected to hand out an annual sum of USD 300-500 million by 2012. In cooperation with the Federal Ministry for Development, during the German G8 Presidency 2007, the World Bank created a "Forest Carbon Partnership Facility," to which Germany has committed EUR 40 million. It is intended to compensate developing countries if they stop felling tropical rainforests.

States have given themselves until the end of 2009 to pave the way for a new climate change agreement. Then they plan to pass the successor to the Kyoto Protocol in Copenhagen. ●

UN Climate Council IPCC
The Intergovernmental Panel on Climate Change (IPCC) is an international group of hundreds of experts and representatives of over 100 states, who analyze climate change on Earth for the United Nations and propose measures to counter it. The fourth report of the IPCC was published in 2007. Fundamentally, it stated that man is exacerbating the greenhouse effect and increasing the temperature of the planet and must take decisive action to counteract these occurrences. Many scientists from Germany have contributed to the UN IPCC's climate report. In late 2007, the UN Climate Panel was awarded the Nobel Peace Prize together with Al Gore. Leading German institutes which focus on climate change include the Max Planck Institute for Meteorology, the Alfred Wegener Institute for Polar and Marine Research, the Wuppertal Institute and the Potsdam Institute for Climate Impact Research.

Joachim Wille
is editor of the politics department and reporter for the daily newspaper "Frankfurter Rundschau."

8

Education, science and research

Germany is a land of ideas. Education, science and research play a central role here. In a Europe free of borders and a world of globalized markets, education lays the basis enabling us to exploit the opportunities open borders and worldwide knowledge networks offer. The German education and university system is undergoing a profound process of renewal that is already bearing fruit: Germany is one of the countries most preferred by foreign students, a hub of cutting-edge international research and a constant source of new patents.

Innovative research: Germany is blazing the way in many technologies of the future

The international competition for the best brains

By Martin Spiewak

FAMED MINDS SUCH AS HUMBOLDT AND EINSTEIN, Hegel and Planck laid the foundations for Germany's reputation as a land of scholars and as the "country of thinkers and poets". As early as medieval times, scholars from all over Europe made the pilgrimage to the newly founded universities in Heidelberg, Cologne and Greifswald. Later, following the university reforms carried out by Wilhelm von Humboldt (1767–1835), the **German universities** actually became considered the ideal example followed by discerning academics elsewhere.

Humboldt conceived of the university as a venue for the independent pursuit of knowledge. It was there that research and teaching were to meld in a single unit, i.e., only those professors were meant to teach students who had themselves through their own research work penetrated to the core of their discipline. Humboldt felt this would guarantee the due depth and breadth of knowledge. At the same time, professors and students were to be free of any state censorship and able to dedicate themselves solely to science and scholarship.

Anyone wanting to make a career for themselves in science had to have spent some time as a student in a German laboratory or lecture hall. In the early 20th century, about one third of all Nobel Prizes were won by German scientists. Their innovations changed the world: the theory of relativity and of nuclear fission, the discovery of the tuberculosis bacillus or of X-rays.

German universities
In Germany there are currently some 1.98 million students enrolled at institutes of higher education, of which 946,000 are women (48 percent). There are 383 such institutes, including 103 universities and 176 universities of the applied sciences. As institutions the state universities are run by the individual federal states. Together with the USA and Great Britain, internationally Germany is one of the most popular countries in which to study.

There are now almost as many female as there are male students

"Heading for the future on the basis of a long-standing tradition": The Ruprecht Karls University in Heidelberg

Among other things, the United States has German researchers to thank for the fact that today it is the leading scientific nation on earth. Hundreds of German scholars, many of them, such as Albert Einstein, Jews, found a new home at an American university or research institute when fleeing the Third Reich. By contrast, for the German research community, their emigration was a severe loss that is still felt today.

Important degrees
Bachelor's
Master's
Diploma
Magister
State examination
Doctorate

Bachelor's and Master's
In many cases in practice both old and new courses and degrees are at present on offer at the same time. In winter semester 2007-8 a total of 6,886 Bachelor's and Master's courses were on offer at German universities, meaning that about 61 % of all courses have now been switched over to the new structure.

Reforms to meet the international competition

Globalization is also creating new challenges for the German scientific and university community. The policymakers and universities have taken the initiative, with a series of reforms to adapt the university system to the new international standards. These innovations are in the process of fundamentally shaking up the German academic world. Be it the switch to staggered **degrees** such as **Bachelor's and Master's** degrees or the introduction of tuition fees and selection tests, be it the emergence of private facilities for academic training or the stronger strategic alliances between universities and institutes outside the higher education system – it is safe to say that hardly a section of

Studying in Germany – the key facts at a glance

The most popular subjects
Of the approx. 300,000 new students enrolled for the winter semester 2006-7, around 146,000 were women

Business administration 22,917
Mechanical Engineering 14,168
German Language and Literature 13,086
Law 11,664
Business Engineering 9,645

Appealing to the international elites of tomorrow
In the winter semester 2006-7, about 250,000 foreign students were enrolled at German universities, and around 55,000 were studying at one of the ten universities most favored by international students:

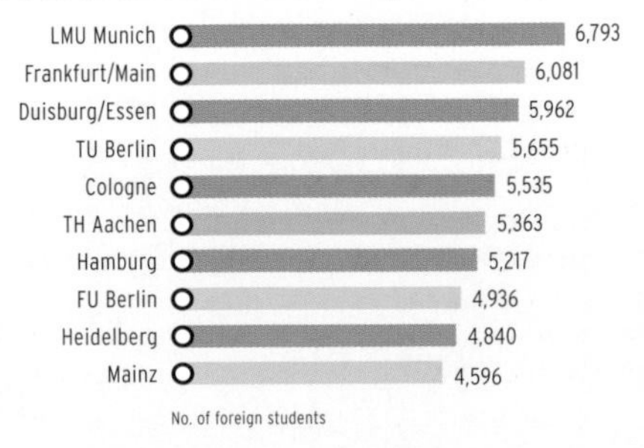

Statistisches Bundesamt, OECD

society is at present undergoing such major changes as is the education system.

The goal of the reforms: to strengthen research and teaching to better face the ever fiercer international competition and to reclaim Germany's leading position. Changed legislation on universities grants each university greater scope, and established professors are being paid more clearly according to their performance. Each big-name university tries to give itself a keener profile, and various **rankings** on university quality and popularity enhance competition.

The so-called "Excellence" initiative for German universities also furthers this goal, too. For five years, the universities selected by an independent group of experts together receive just short of EUR 2 billion. The money is dedicated to promoting post-grad schemes, outstanding centers in specific fields of research (excellence clusters) and the research portfolios of nine top universities. This "elite" includes the LMU and TU in Munich, TU Karlsruhe, RWTH Aachen and the universities of Konstanz, Göttingen, Heidelberg, Freiburg, and the FU Berlin.

The **German Research Foundation** (DFG) is the main financial backer and primarily responsible for organizing

University ranking
Oldest university: Ruprecht Karls University, Heidelberg, founded in 1386
Biggest university: Cologne University, with 45,600 students
Most attractive university for top international research: University of Bayreuth, according to the Alexander von Humboldt Foundation-based research ranking
Universities with greatest research activities: Technical University of Munich and the University of Heidelberg according to CHE research ranking
Biggest private university: Catholic University of Eichstätt-Ingolstadt with 4,800 students

German Research Foundation (Deutsche Forschungsgemeinschaft)
The DFG is science's central self-governing organization. It supports research projects, whereby funds are channeled primarily into institutes of higher education. It also promotes collaboration between researchers and advises parliaments and authorities.

Most popular countries to study in
Worldwide a good 2.73 million students attend foreign universities . Germany is one of the most popular places to study

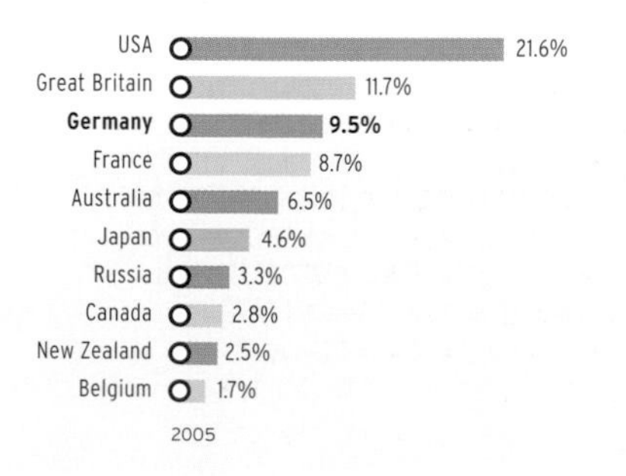

Increasingly international degrees
Most students opt to graduate with a Magister or a Diploma, but Bachelor's and Master's programs are becoming ever more popular

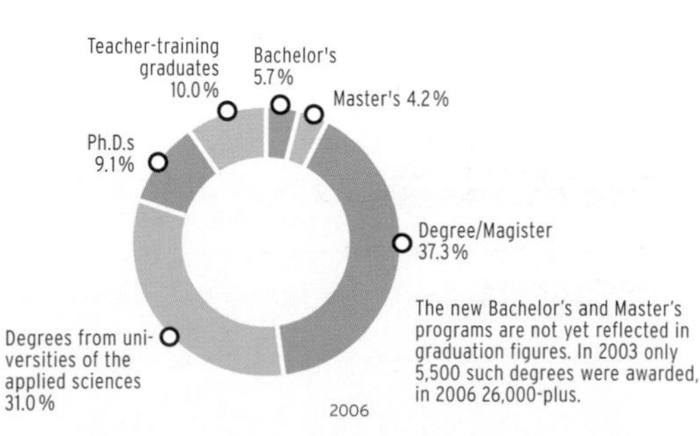

this Excellence Initiative. One section of the latter in particular promises to have a long-term impact: The idea is to reward reform concepts put forward by a university and outlining how in the years to come it intends to emerge at the pinnacle of international **research**. In other words, gone are the days when the university system was based on largely egalitarian principles and research and teaching were essentially on an equal footing in every German university.

Research at higher education institutes
Based on the principle of "the unity of research and teaching", German universities are not only establishments for teaching students, but are also engaged in top-level research. A pre-requisite for this is close collaboration between scientists and research institutes both inside and outside Germany. The universities are financed by public funds, foundations and research work commissioned by third parties.

The tertiary education system

After the Second World War, an academic community arose that was more broadly diversified than ever before, a fact stimulated by German reunification in 1990. Anyone wanting to study in Germany is able to choose between 383 higher-education institutions that are spread across the entire country. Be it in cities or in the countryside, traditional or highly modern, small with everything in walk-

School education

Good initial opportunities for everyone are a key prerequisite for education and achievement. German schooling is based on nine years of compulsory education for all children. Attendance of all government schools is free of charge. Once children are aged six, they as a rule attend primary school for four years, before going on to a variety of secondary schools: Hauptschule, Realschule, Gymnasium. The standards and weighting of practical versus theoretical lessons differ. There are also Gesamtschulen, in which all children of compulsory school age are taught in parallel classes, depending on their particular abilities. Children can easily move from one stream to another as they improve. In Hauptschulen, grades 5 to 9 are compulsory, and 10th grade is voluntary. Realschule covers grades 5 to 10 and is halfway between Hauptschule and a Gymnasium. The children leave with a "Mittlere Reife" certificate. Gymnasium provides in-depth education. Pupils graduate from Gymnasium after the 12th or 13th grade with a High-School Certificate.
Lessons in German schools tend to be in the mornings but the Federal Government has provided EUR 4 billion to support the creation of all-day schools. Since 2003, this money has been used to support more than 6,000 schools in effort to upgrade or establish day-long instruction. Forward-looking support at the pre-school level and more language classes are likewise intended to enhance the quality of education. A Standing Conference of the Ministers of Education and Cultural Affairs of the Länder coordinates schooling, as each Federal state has its own school laws.

ing distance or large and spread across a pulsating metropolis – today almost every larger German city has its own college or university. The state of North Rhine-Westphalia alone has over 15 universities, 27 universities of the applied sciences and 8 art academies. Many of them were founded in the 1960s and 1970s, the age of major expansion in tertiary education, when within the space of only two decades, the number of students exploded by a factor of five, with the figure for female students rocketing most. Today, they have almost overtaken the number of their male counterparts.

Today, some two million young people study in Germany. More than one third of every age set enters tertiary education, and the ratio is growing. Nevertheless, Germany is still below the international average, firstly owing to the relatively low ratio of pupils who obtain a high-school leaver's certificate and secondly as just one third of the latter group opt for vocational training in the tried-and-true dual system (see p. 129). This provides training for many professions that would require a university degree in other countries – such as for crafts/technical careers or for technical and auxiliary medical jobs.

Again, unlike many other countries, **private universities** play a comparatively subordinate role: 96 percent of students attend public institutions that are subject to state supervision and control and are essentially open to anyone who has a high-school leaver's certificate (or a comparable certificate) that authorizes them to enter university. Since the 1970s, alongside the state universities and theological colleges, countless non-state-funded, non-denominational universities have been founded, financed by tuition fees and donations.

A university degree – the launchpad for a successful career

Private universities
In addition to the non-state funded, denominational institutes of higher education, a number of state-recognized, private educational establishments have been founded since the 1970s. There are now 110 - mostly small - non state-funded higher education institutes, including 13 private universities such as the European Business School in Oestrich-Winkel, and the Private University of Witten/Herdecke, as well as 15 theological universities.

Technical universities and universities of the applied sciences

While the classic university is dedicated to pure science and scholarship and covers the entire spectrum from ancient

Inventions and Innovations

The ideas country: From the bicycle to the MP3 format – German inventors and inventions shape today's world. Innovations "made in Germany" at a glance

1796
Homeopathy
Heal a disease with something similar to it: This was the idea **Samuel Hahnemann** (1755-1843) used to create the principle of homeopathic therapy. Today, just under 40 percent of Germans have used this soft form of medicine

1854
Light bulb
The clockmaker was well ahead of his day. For in 1854, when **Heinrich Göbel** (1818-1893) caused bamboo fibers to glow in a vacuum, there was still no electrical grid. Today, some 350 million light bulbs are sold each year

1760 1780 1800 1820 1840

18th century

19th

1817
The bicycle
Karl von Drais (1785-1851) was especially taken by the "two-wheeler principle". The bicycle was soon to become a success story world-wide

1861
Telephone
The era of revolutionary communications technology commenced with **Philipp Reis** (1834-1874). A mathematics teacher, he was the first person to transform sounds and words into electric current that could be reproduced elsewhere

1876
Refrigerator
On March 25, 1876 **Carl von Linde** (1842-1934) was awarded the patent for the first refrigerator, which used ammonia as a cooling agent. In 1993, German company **Foron** introduced the world's first CFC-free "Greenfreeze" refrigerator

1930/1931
Television
On Christmas Eve, 1930 **Manfred von Ardenne** (1907-1997) was the first person to succeed with an electrical television broadcast. Today, 95 percent of German households have a TV. Average viewing time per day is about 220 minutes

1876
Otto engine
Take in, condense, ignite, work, expel: **Nikolaus August Otto** (1832-1891) has gone down in the annals of technology as the inventor of the four-stroke engine, accelerating the pace of motorization

1891
Glider
He realized one of mankind's oldest dreams: In 1891, **Otto Lilienthal** (1848-1896) managed in gliding in the air for 25 meters. Today, some 7,850 unmotorized gliders sail in Germany's skies

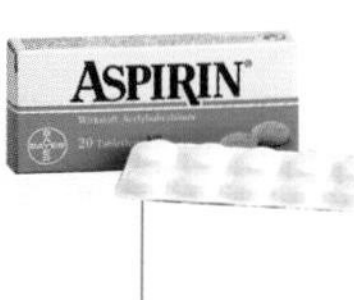

1897
Aspirin
On August 10, 1897 chemist **Felix Hoffmann** (1868-1946) synthesized a white powder that was soon to prove to be a "miracle treatment": acetyl salicylic acid

1885
Automobile
They made society mobile: **Carl Benz** (1844-1929) and **Gottlieb Daimler** (1834-1900). Today, over 46 million automobiles are registered in Germany

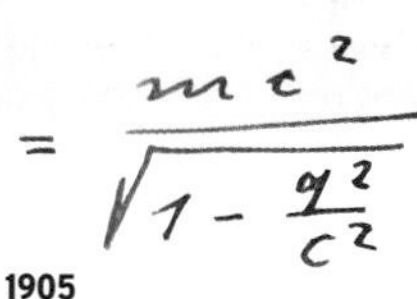

1905
Theory of relativity
He did not develop a product or invent a process. Instead he created a new idea of time and space. **Albert Einstein** (1879-1955), who emigrated from Germany in 1933, was the first pop star of science. His formula read: $E=mc^2$

Innovations "made in Germany"

1957
Rawl plugs
Simple but ingenious: This is the only way to describe the invention of the plastic rawl plug. For "patents world champion" **Artur Fischer** the patent for his rawl plug was only one of over 5,000 that he has accumulated during his long life as an entrepreneur

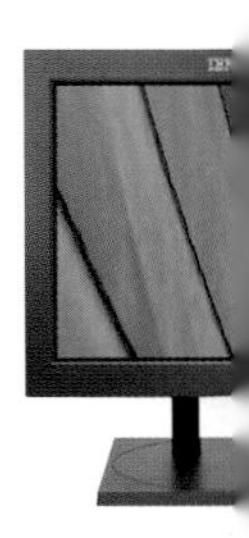

1939
Jet engine
As a student **Hans von Ohain** (1911-1998) was already hunting for a new engine for aircraft. His vision: "thrust" was to be provided by propulsion. In 1939, the first jet airplane took off in Rostock

1969
Chipcard
Under Patent DE 19 45777 C3 **Jürgen Dethloff** (1924-2002) and **Helmut Gröttrup** (1916-1981) opened the door wide to the information society. As a check card, phone card or patient card, today, your chipcard is a firm part of everyday life

1940 1950 1960 1970

20th century

1941
Computer
Because he did not like maths tasks, **Konrad Zuse** (1910-1995) invented the first binary calculator: the Z3. The first computer managed four basic arithmetic functions in three seconds. It was the beginning of the digital age. Today, 240 million PCs are sold each year, alone eight million of them in Germany

1963
Scanner
The inventor of the precursor to fax machines **Rudolf Hell** (1901-2002) had first thought of dividing texts and images into dots and lines back in the 1920s. His Hell telegraph system was the first to transfer texts and images over long distances. In 1963, he invented the first scanner for inputting color images

1979
Magnetic levitation railway
The world's first maglev ran in Hamburg. Today, the German "Transrapid" travels at 430 kph from Shanghai airport to the CBD. The ingenious idea for magnetic levitation dates back to work in 1933 by engineer **Hermann Kemper** (1892-1977)

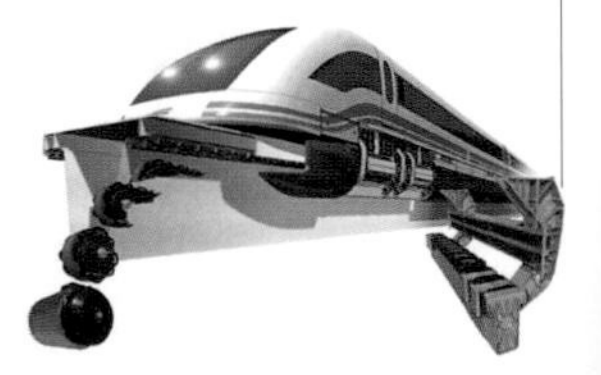

1995
MP3
For millions of kids today, MP3 players are simply the best. This method of audio compression was developed by a team at the Fraunhofer Institute under **Karlheinz Brandenburg**

2005
Airbus A 380
A European success story with a lot of German technology: the **Airbus A 380** is the world's largest airliner. Spring 2005 saw the maiden flight of the giant of the air

2007
Hard disk revolution
Nine years after the discovery of the giant magnetoresistance effect, Jülich-based physicist **Peter Grünberg** and Frenchman Albert Fert won the Nobel Prize for Physics.

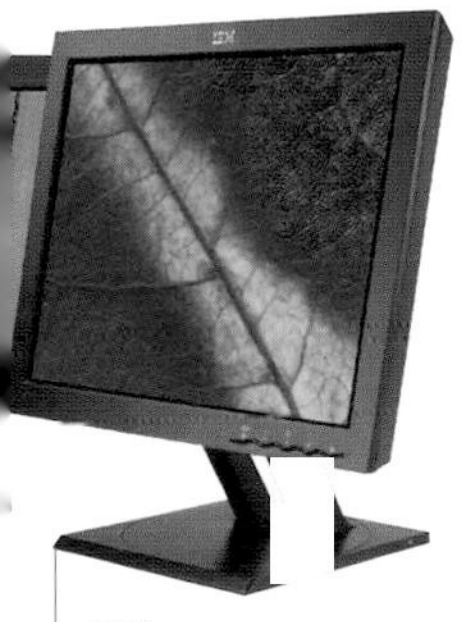

1976
Liquid crystal display
The future of monitors is large and flat thanks to modern liquid crystals. Darmstadt-based company Merck was the first to offer them for sale, in 1904. The breakthrough came in 1976 with substances with enhanced optical and chemical display properties

1994
Fuel cell automobile
As early as 1838, **Christian Friedrich Schönbein** (1799-1868) developed the principle of the fuel cell. But not until 1994 did Daimler-Benz AG exploit its potential for the world's first fuel-cell powered car

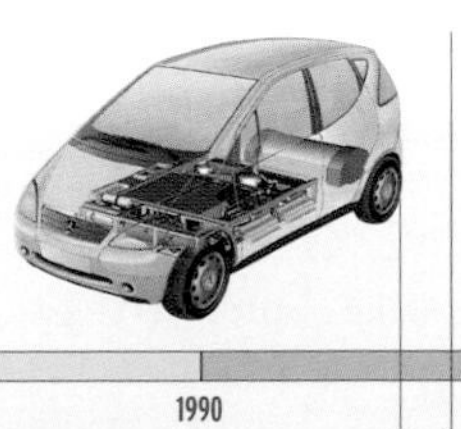

1980 1990 2000 2010

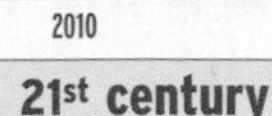

1986
Scanning tunnel microscope
It renders even atoms, the smallest pieces of matter, visible. German **Gerd Binnig** and Swiss **Heinrich Rohrer** were awarded the Nobel Prize for Physics for their invention in 1986. It was the decisive breakthrough into the nanoworld

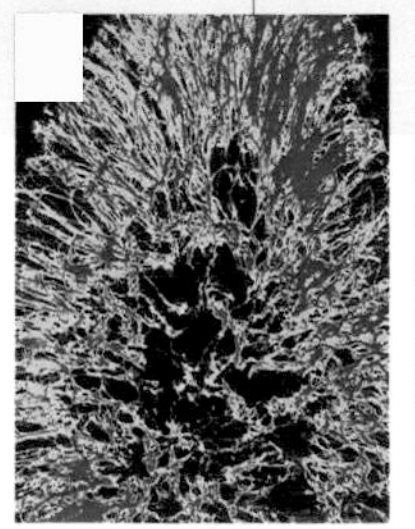

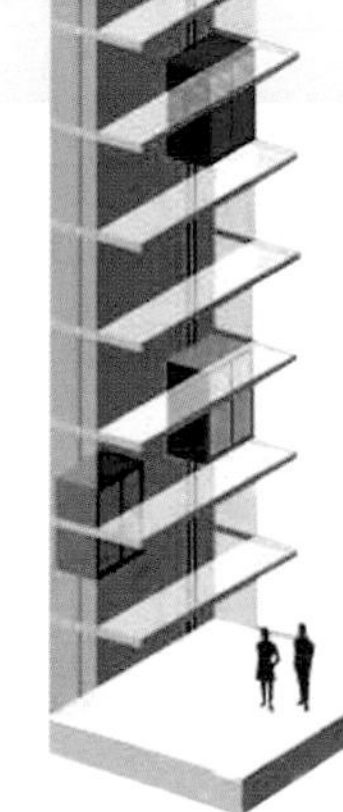

2002
Twin elevators
How can two elevator cabins move independently in one and the same shaft? They can thanks to a hypermodern control mechanism by the **Thyssen Krupp** company. Twin elevators create a new dimension in facilities management

Wilhelm von Humboldt: In Germany, he established the university as a home for the independent pursuit of knowledge

studies through to economics, the **technical universities** (TU) focus on engineering and the natural sciences. The TUs have a sterling reputation as the forges of German engineering know-how and are especially popular among foreign students.

Since the late 1960s, another special institution has evolved in the German education system: the university of the applied sciences (FH). More than a quarter of all students in Germany attend a FH, or a so-called vocational academy as it is known in some German states – these collaborate closely with corporations. Students are attracted to the universities of the applied sciences above all by the fact that the track to a job is shorter – an FH degree course lasts three years as a rule – and the curriculum is more practically oriented. Stringently organized courses and regular examinations ensure that the average time spent obtaining a degree is less. This does not mean that there is any shortfall in scholarship – the approx. 176 universities of the applied sciences also conduct research, albeit with a strong focus on potential applications and industry's needs.

Technical universities
Universities with an especially strong technical focus operate as Technical Universities (TU) or Technical Colleges (TH). They attach greater importance to basic research than do universities of applied science. The nine leading TUs have joined ranks to form the TU9 Initiative. They have an especially strong international focus and coordinate their countless study export offerings outside Germany.

Internationalization
There are currently 250,000 foreign students enrolled at German higher education institutes, of whom approximately one in four gained the right to study there in Germany itself. However, there are also some 76,000 Germans studying abroad. The most popular countries are Holland, Great Britain, Austria and the USA.

International Orientation

Germany appeals to young people from all over the world as a place to study. About 250,000 foreign students are enrolled at German universities, 70 percent more than in

1995. Today, more than every tenth student comes from abroad, the largest numbers coming from eastern Europe and China. Germany is the third most preferred host country for international students, following the United States and Great Britain.

This success German universities have had in **internationalization** is the product of the joint efforts of each and every university and politicians. Thus, an image campaign for German universities was launched a few years ago together with university organizations. Moreover, with government support several universities have participated in founding partner universities in other countries, including Singapore (TU Munich), Cairo (Ulm and Stuttgart universities) and Seoul (the Weimar Academy of Music). As a rule, the **DAAD**, German Academic Exchange Service, lead manages such foreign initiatives – it is dedicated to international exchange programs for students and scientists alike, and supports offices, lecturers or alumni associations in over 100

DAAD
The German Academic Exchange Service (DAAD) is an organization run jointly by the German institutes of higher education. Its purpose is to promote relations between higher education institutes in Germany and abroad, especially through exchange schemes between students and academics. As a rule its programs cover all disciplines and countries and are open to German and foreign students in equal measure. The DAAD supports a worldwide network of offices, lecturers and alumni associations and provides information and advice on a local basis.

Two-track vocational training

Germany's two-track vocational training system is quite special internationally speaking. On completing school, some 60 percent of young people in Germany move on to learn one of the 350 officially recognized vocations included in the Two-Track System. This entry into professional life differs from vocational training based only in colleges such as customary in many other countries. The practical part of the course takes part on 3 or 4 days of the week in a company; the other 1 or 2 days are spent with specialist theoretical instruction in a vocational school. The courses take 2-3.5 years. In-company training is supported by courses and additional qualification facilities outside the companies. Training is financed by the companies, which pay the trainees/apprentices wages, while the government bears the costs of the vocational schools. At present, 482,000 companies, the public sector and the free professions are busy training young people. Small and medium-sized business provide more than 80 percent of all traineeships. Thanks to the Two-Track System, in Germany the number of young people without a profession or traineeship is comparatively low, and is only 2.3 percent of those in the 15-19 age bracket. This combination of theory and practical work guarantees that the craftsmen and skilled workers have prime qualifications. Vocational training is also a launchpad for a career that can, via advanced training, lead to participants becoming master craftsmen and women. A new qualification track: advanced training alongside the job that can lead even as far as a university Master's degree.

Bologna Declaration
In 1999 in Bologna, Germany, together with its European neighbors, set itself the target of establishing a common European university system by the year 2010. This reform has resulted in the transformation of degree courses into the two-tier Bachelor's and Master's degree courses and the introduction of credits in accordance with a system that is recognized throughout Europe.

Albert Einstein revolutionized our understanding of time and space

countries. It also played a role in setting up hundreds of foreign-language courses (frequently in English) at German universities.

Moreover, an increasing number of departments are switching their courses over to culminate in internationally recognized Bachelor's and Master's degrees. By 2010, all universities should have adopted this new degree policy – as stipulated in the **"Bologna Declaration"**, to which all European states are signatories. The idea is not only to facilitate student exchanges throughout the continent, but also to make Europe a more interesting prospect for overseas academics.

What has long since been the norm at art and music academies is, according to the plan, in future also to be the practice at every university. Until recently, only a small number of departments chose their own students. A central office, the ZVS, handles allocation to universities of students to those subjects with **admission restrictions** – nationwide these are at present Biology, Medicine, Pharmacology, Psychology, Veterinary Medicine and Dental Medicine (and there are also special state-wide restrictions in North Rhine-Westphalia). An increasing number of universities are also issuing their own specific restrictions, and first testing or interviewing applicants before awarding them places.

German Nobel Prize winners in the natural sciences and medicine

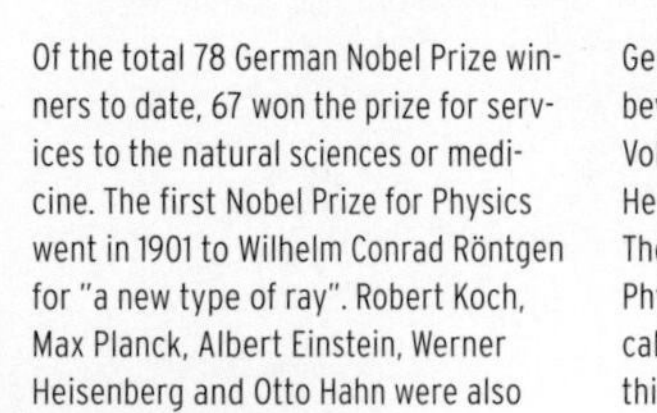

Of the total 78 German Nobel Prize winners to date, 67 won the prize for services to the natural sciences or medicine. The first Nobel Prize for Physics went in 1901 to Wilhelm Conrad Röntgen for "a new type of ray". Robert Koch, Max Planck, Albert Einstein, Werner Heisenberg and Otto Hahn were also German Nobel Prize winners famed well beyond their field. Christiane Nüsslein-Volhard (Medicine), Horst L. Störmer, Herbert Kroemer, Wolfgang Ketterle and Theodor Hänsch, Peter Grünberg (all Physics) as well as Gerhard Ertl (Chemicals) were recent German winners of this pinnacle of scientific recognition.

1	**1901**	**Conrad Röntgen**
2	**1905**	**Robert Koch**
3	**1932**	**Werner Heisenberg**
4	**1995**	**Chr. Nüsslein-Volhard**
5	**1998**	**Horst L. Störmer**
6	**2000**	**Herbert Kroemer**
7	**2001**	**Wolfgang Ketterle**
8	**2007**	**Gerhard Ertl**

In 2005, a Federal Constitutional Court ruling overturned the traditional taboo on tuition fees. Hitherto, in Germany it was (almost) only the state that paid for tertiary education. Since 2007, seven federal states have from the first semester onwards charged **tuition fees**, albeit relatively modest ones by international comparison. Other Federal states also levy tuition fees for students who have exceeded ten semesters or have opted after graduation to study another subject.

Research in industry

While it is the universities that are solely responsible for courses of study, needless to say in Germany research is also undertaken outside the university. Thus, German industry is strongly engaged in research: Germany easily outpaced the other European countries in the league table, with 24,000 registrations for patents submitted to the European Patent Office. In the form of Siemens, Bosch and BASF, three German corporations are among the world's Top 7 in the international patent registration league table. Germany is also well up in the global patent registration rankings for applied technologies such as automobile, mechanical, environmental, chemical, power and construction technologies. As regards registrations of

Admission restrictions
Given immense demand for some courses, nationwide admission restrictions (numerus clausus) hold. Since 2005, degree courses subject to national admission restrictions are subject to proportional entry ("20-20-60"): 20 percent of places go to students with the best high school leavers' certificates, who can chose a university, and 20 percent are allocated on the basis of how long students have been waiting for a place. Universities can restrict access to 60 percent of places by both average school leaver's certificate grades and criteria of their own.

Tuition fees
Since 2007, the Federal states of Baden-Württemberg, Bavaria, Hamburg, Hessen, Lower Saxony, North Rhine-Westphalia and Saarland levy tuition fees as of enrollment. Most have set the fees at EUR 500 per semester, but offer secured loans to finance them.

Leading the Patents table
The total of 135,183 registrations for patents with the European Patents Office in 2006 can be subdivided as follows

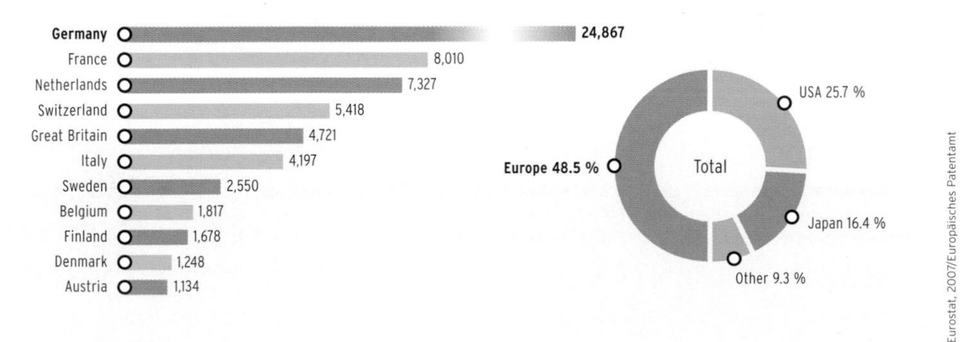

Max Planck Society
The Max Planck Society was founded on February 26, 1948 - as the successor to the Kaiser Wilhelm Society set up in 1911 for the promotion of science. Max Planck Institutes undertake basic research in the natural sciences, bio-sciences and social sciences as well as the humanities. Together with partner universities, MPG has founded 49 postgraduate and international Max-Planck Research Schools. Half of the doctoral students come from outside Germany.

Fraunhofer-Gesellschaft
The society is engaged in applied research. Its projects are commissioned by industry and service providers as well as state-run institutions. Some 12,500 members of staff are employed in around 56 research facilities throughout the whole of Germany. The amount spent on research annually totals EUR 1.2 billion. Fraunhofer supports offices in Europe, the USA, Asia, and the Middle East.

patents for environmental protection, Germany leads the way world-wide, followed by the USA and Japan.

Research outside the universities

Cutting-edge research is also being done at hundreds of scientific institutes that are grouped together in organizations such as the Helmholtz Association, the Fraunhofer-Gesellschaft and the Leibniz Association. Precisely these research institutes outside the universities offer leading research minds optimal working conditions that are as good as unparalleled the world over. Here, some of the most fruitful German minds are busy undertaking research and publishing highly original articles. This is especially true of the 78 Max Planck Institutes (MPI). Be it searching for water on Mars, the human genome project, or exploring human behavior, the MPIs are at the forefront of things when it comes to exploring virgin scientific terrain. Since the Max Plank Society was founded in 1948 its scientists have won 17 Nobel Prizes and many other international awards. In 2007, the Nobel Prize for Chemistry was won by MPI Director Gerhard Ertl. The **Max Planck Society** is so appealing to them because of how it sees research: Each institute defines its own topics, is equipped with superb working conditions, and has a free hand when selecting staff. For many a scholar, being appointed Director of an MPI is the pinnacle of his or her career.

The topic on the Internet

www.das-ranking.de
DAAD, the CHE Centrum für Hochschulentwicklung and "DIE ZEIT" offer a database with a detailed ranking of German universities (English, German)

www.bildungsserver.de
The information portal on the German education system (German, English)

www.hochschulkompass.de
This Web site offers information on university study, Ph.D. courses and international collaboration in Germany (English, German)

www.forschungsportal.net
Search engine run by the Federal Ministry of Research on research findings, Ph.D. theses (English, German)

www.dfg.de
Information on the German Research Foundation (English, German)

www.daad.de, www.studieren-in.de
The German Academic Exchange Service Web site provides information for foreign students in Germany and on scholarships (in 24 languages)

What is rare at an MPI is by contrast the very source of life for the **Fraunhofer-Gesellschaft** institutes, namely close collaboration with industry. There are about 80 such research facilities, and they conduct applied research primarily into engineering-related fields. Fraunhofer experts have one foot in the lab and the other in the factory, as their projects are as a rule commissioned by companies, specifically mid-sized corporations.

The 83 member institutes of the **Leibniz-Gemeinschaft** are not only strong in the life and natural sciences, but also trend-setters in the humanities, the social sciences and economics. They include ifo-Institut für Wirtschaftsforschung, which regularly publishes a business climate index, Deutsches Museum in Munich, one of the world's leading science and technology museums, the Bernhard Nocht Institute for Tropical Medicine in Hamburg, and Mannheim's Institute of German Language, that provides scholarly support for advances to the German language.

A total of 15 high-tech German research facilities are joined under the aegis of the **Helmholtz Association**; they are large and often extremely expensive institutions that are well known internationally, such as the Gesellschaft für Schwerionenforschung (GSI), the German Cancer Research Center (DKFZ), the Deutsche Elektronen-Synchrotron in Hamburg (DESY) or the Alfred Wegener Institute for Polar and Marine Research in Bremerhaven. Every year, the Helmholtz institutes attract thousands of foreign researchers, who wish to conduct physical or medical experiments in what are often facilities that are unique worldwide.

The Federal Government has a policy of targeted support with which it wishes to get Germany moving forward faster. Through 2010 three percent of GDP will be committed to R&D (2005: 2.51 percent). Moreover, the funding for research institutes will by raised by three percent annually through 2010 and EUR 6 billion will be invested in nano-, bio- and information technology. ●

Leibniz-Gemeinschaft
Gottfried Wilhelm Leibniz (1646–1716) was one of the last all-round scholars. The scientific range covered by the 83 member institutes is correspondingly broad, extending from the humanities and economics through to mathematics. The focus is on applied basic research. The Leibniz institutes employ more than 13,000 staff and have a total budget of about EUR 1.1 billion.

Helmholtz Association
With 15 research centers, an annual budget of around EUR 2.3 billion and 26,500 members of staff the Helmholtz Association is Germany's largest scientific organization. It conducts research into energy, the earth and the environment, health, key technologies, the structure of material as well as traffic and outer space.

Martin Spiewak
The journalist is the scientific editor of "Die Zeit", a German weekly.

9

Society

Germany has about 82 million inhabitants. It is by far the largest country in the EU in terms of population. Germany is a modern, cosmopolitan country. Its society is shaped by a plurality of life styles and truly different ethno-cultural diversity. Forms of coexistence have become more varied, and the scope individuals enjoy has become greater. Traditional gender roles have been dispensed with. Despite the social changes, the family remains the most important social reference unit and young people have very close bonds with their parents.

German society - modern, pluralist and open-minded

By Rainer Geißler

GERMAN SOCIETY IS A MODERN, open-minded society: Most people – both young and old – are well-educated and enjoy a high **standard of living**, as well as sufficient freedom to be able to plan their lives as they themselves see fit. The nucleus of their lives is the family, which is constantly adopting new forms. Yet society is faced with the challenge of solving important problems such as population trends – the ageing of society as well as immigration, which is increasingly varied in terms of ethnic culture. And there is one thing the Germans still have to overcome: the effects of the 45 years during which the country was divided. Since political reunification in 1990 much has happened, and yet restoring the social unity of Germany will remain an important issue for the foreseeable future.

Standard of living
Germany is one of the countries with the highest standard of living in the world. According to the UN's HDI Index, Germany is one of the most developed countries in the world in terms of life expectancy, degree of literacy and per-capita income. The healthcare system enables comprehensive medical care, whereby the social security systems of the statutory health insurances, care and accident insurance and unemployment support protect people against existential risks.

Population

With reunification Germany became the country with by far the largest population in the European Union. Around 82 million people live on German territory, almost one fifth of them in what was formerly East Germany. Three trends are characteristic of demographic developments in Germany: a low birth rate, increasing life expectancy and an ageing society.

For 30 years now Germany has been witnessing few births: With slight fluctuations, since 1975 the number of newborn infants has been approximately 1.3 chil-

Life expectancy
While the average life expectancy in the early 20th century was about 46, a boy born today can expect to reach the age of 77 and a girl as much as 82.

dren per woman. This means that for 30 years the generation of children has been smaller than that of their parents. High rates of immigration to Germany from other societies prevented the overall population from shrinking accordingly. At the same time life expectancy has risen continuously, and is now 77 years for men and 82 years for women.

The rise in **life expectancy** and, to an even greater extent, the low birth rates are the reason for the third trend: The ratio of young people in the overall population is decreasing, that of elderly people rising: In the early 1990s there were almost three people of an employable age for every person over the age of 60. In the early 21st century, the ratio was only 1 to 2.2 and calculations indicate that within the next decade the ratio will already be less than 1 to 2. The ageing of society is one of the greatest challenges facing welfare and family policy. For this reason the pension insurance scheme has been undergoing re-structured for some time

A sporting nation

In 2006, Germany and guests from all over the world celebrated a "summer fairytale": The World Cup kindled a marvelous mood in the stadiums and streets among fans and others alike. And a continuation beckons soon: In 2011, the FIFA Women's World Cup will be held in Germany, which is the defending champion. And the event is bound to be another great football party. As will be the IAAF 2009 Athletics World Championships in Berlin. Football is Germany's no. 1 sport: with more than 6.5 million people in 26,000 clubs, DFB, the German Football Association, is the world's largest sports association. And it is especially young people who are active: More than 2.3 million boys and girls play football in the 21 state federations. Their goal: the Bundesliga, one of Europe's strongest leagues. DFB is a member of DOSB, the German Olympic Sports Confederation, which with its 27-million-odd members in 90,000 clubs is the world's largest sports organization. DOSB supports not only high-performance but also mass sports. The best-loved leisure time sports are, other than football, gymnastics, tennis, shooting, athletics and handball. This sporting enthusiasm constantly produces new leading sports personalities who are at the forefront of things at the European and World Championships, not to mention the Olympic Games. Germans are especially successful in the fields of athletics, swimming, rowing, canooing, and riding. And Germany is one of the leading nations in the all-time medals table.

now: The traditional **"cross-generational contract"** is becoming less and less affordable, such that private individuals are supplementing it by making their own provisions for old age. In addition, family-related measures to increase the number of children are also being implemented.

Families

The family is still the first and most important social group of people and one of the most significant social institutions. Over the years its importance as the nucleus of life has if anything increased rather than decreased. For almost 90 percent of the population the family comes first in their list of personal priorities. Young people also value it very highly: 72 percent of 12 to 25-year olds are of the opinion that being happy is dependent on having a family.

Yet ideas about what form families should take, as well as their structure, have changed dramatically in the wake of social change. In the traditional family, the roles played by a couple that was married for life, and bringing up several children, were strictly divided: the father was the breadwinner, the mother a housewife. This "breadwinner" model is certainly still lived out – for example in the lower social classes, by migrants, or for a certain period of time, as long as the children are still small – but it is no longer the predominant way of life.

A far wider range of forms of cohabitation has emerged. There is now far greater leeway in choosing between various family forms and even deciding not to have a family at all. This is in no small way connected to the altered role women play: Nowadays some 64 percent of mothers are in employment. Families have become smaller. There are more instances of single-child families than those with three or more children. Two-child families are typical. There are also increasing numbers of people living alone or as a couple with no children. Almost one third of women born in 1965 still have no children today.

Cross-generational contract
This is the name of the system used to finance statutory pension insurance: employees today pay proportional contributions toward the pensions of the generation of retirees in the expectation that the coming generation will then pay for their pensions. The first mandatory regulations on old-age security were made as long ago as 1889. Today about 80 percent of employed persons pay into the statutory pension system. Alongside contributions by the employers and employees, today the system is also funded by government subsidies. Since 2002, statutory pensions have been supplemented by state-supported, private capital-backed old-age provisions. In addition to the state pension for employees, other forms of pensions and insurances secure old age provisions for civil servants and the self-employed.

The family continues to be the key social institution

Ways of life
There are many different ways of life in Germany, but most people, or almost 67 million, live in multi-person households, and 16 million live on their own. More than 42 million live as parent/child combinations, including about 20 million children. Just short of 23 million people live as couples, but without children. The latter includes primarily 39,000 men and 23,000 women who live in a home with their same-sex partners. In total, there are estimated to be some 160,000 same-sex partnerships in Germany.

Single parents
In around 90 percent of the 1.6-million families in which a single parent brings up the children, that person is the mother. Many of them are not employed or work part-time. In order to make it easier for them to work, the plan is to further improve all-day care for children and care facilities for the under-3s.

Not only the **ways of life**, but also basic moral attitudes are undergoing change. Faithfulness to one's partner remains an important value, but the norm of staying together for life has become more relaxed. The expectations associated of a partnership, on the other hand, have risen. This is one of the reasons for some 40 percent of marriages over the past few years ending in divorce. As a rule most people marry again of find another partner. There has also been a marked increase in the number of couples living out of wedlock.

This form of cohabitation without actually being officially married is particularly popular with young people and those whose marriage has recently failed. As a result the number of illegitimate children has also risen: In West Germany about a quarter and in East Germany more than half of all children are born to unwed mothers. One result of this change is an increase in the number of step-parents and single-parent families: One fifth of all households with children have **single parents**, and as a rule these are single mothers.

Over the past few decades the relations within families themselves have also progressed. As a rule the relationship between parents and children is exceedingly good and for the most part is no longer characterized by obedience, subordination and dependence but rather by involvement and equal rights, support, affection and being brought up to be independent.

Despite the fact that nowadays instances of three generations of one family living under the same roof are very rare, there are strong emotional bonds between grown-up children and their parents and between grandparents and their grandchildren.

Women and men

In Germany, as in other modern societies, there has been tremendous progress with regard to the **equal rights** for women stipulated in the Basic Law. As such, with regard to education girls have not only drawn level with, but have indeed now overtaken boys. At grammar schools they account for 56 percent of graduates; the share of young women embarking on degree courses at university totals almost 54 percent. Of the apprentices who passed their final examination in 2006, 43 percent were young women. And more and more women are embarking on careers. And the alimony laws in the case of divorce in force from 2008 make it all the more important for women to be employed. Nowadays 67 percent of women in Western Germany and 73 percent in Eastern Germany work. Whereas as a rule men are in full-time employment women, especially those with small children, work part time.

Equal rights

In Germany, equal rights are enshrined in the Basic Law, it is legally impermissible to discriminate by gender as regards working conditions and pay, and there are numerous laws guaranteeing the rights of women. Moreover, Germany is firmly committed to equal rights for both genders - relying on a wide-ranging network of state and private institutions in this regard. With the introduction of gender mainstreaming, women's politics has been integrated as a cross-disciplinary function into all government and local departments and agencies. Thus, the state is proactively advancing the creation of equal conditions for men and women. These measures are being successful: Germany places 9th best world-wide in the UN's GEM Index which measures women's participation in business and politics.

Women in Germany

Girls with the best education

In recent years, major steps have been taken to ensure not only equal rights, but also factual equal opportunities for women. For many women, having a job is very important. Two thirds of women are now in gainful employment, and this figure does not change greatly if they become mothers. Great progress has been made in training and education for girls - the key basis for their finding jobs. The number of young women holding higher qualifications and degree is now higher than that of their male counterparts.

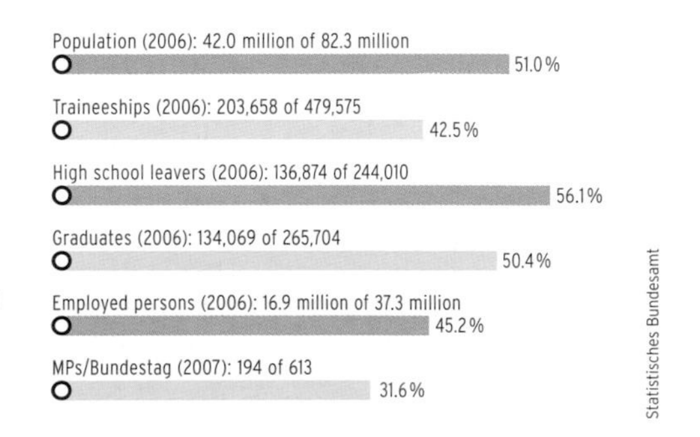

Living in Germany

Work and leisure time, family and commitment: How Germans structure their everyday life, how they spend their time, what is important to them and things they support

High proportion of women in employment

In Germany there are some 37 million people in employment, of which 7.4 million live in the new federal states and 17 million female. Women now account for 45 percent of those in employment – in Eastern Germany as much as 47 percent. In other words, about 68 percent of employable women are in jobs

Trend to more part-time work

More and more people are working part time: In spring 2006 these totaled 8.6 million, and now account for 26.2 percent of those working for an employer. The majority of those in part-time employment are women – mostly mothers – who do 82 percent of all such jobs. This results in average weekly working hours for men of over 40 hours, and for women of only just 30 hours

Statistisches Bundesamt

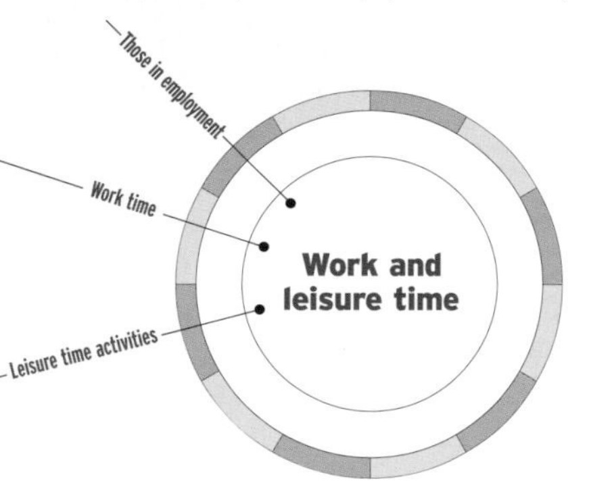

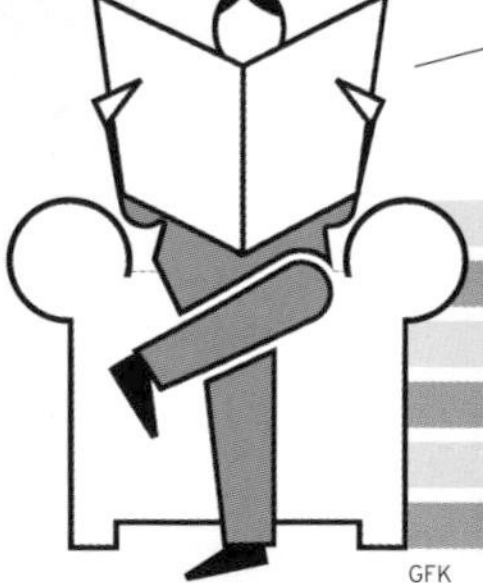

The most popular leisure time activities (in percent)

Activity	Percent
Relaxing at home	70
DIY/gardening	38
Going out	38
Sport	25
Cinema	25
Culture	15

GFK

Almost one in three people lives in a big city

Germany is one of the most densely populated countries in the world. Munich has almost 4,200 and Berlin 3,800 inhabitants per square kilometer, while in Mecklenburg-Western Pomerania there are only 73. Around 29 million persons or a good 35 percent, lives in small towns of up to 20,000 inhabitants. More than 30 percent live in big cities with a population of more than 100,000, of which there are 82 in Germany

Six hours leisure time

Nowadays people in Germany have more leisure time than ten years ago – on average around six hours a day. They prefer spending this time at home, and relax for some two hours watching TV or listening to music. Men have almost half an hour more leisure time than women

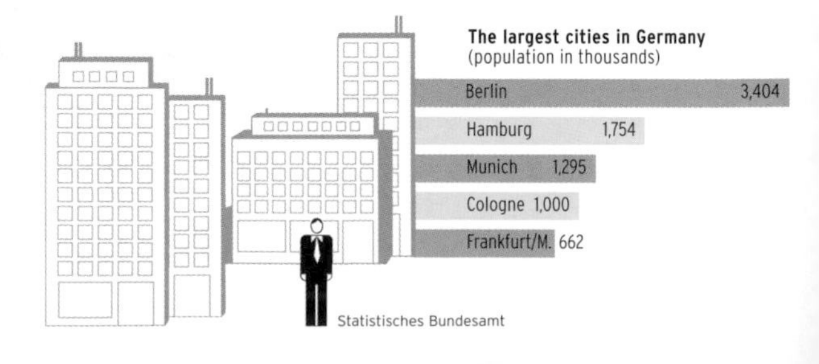

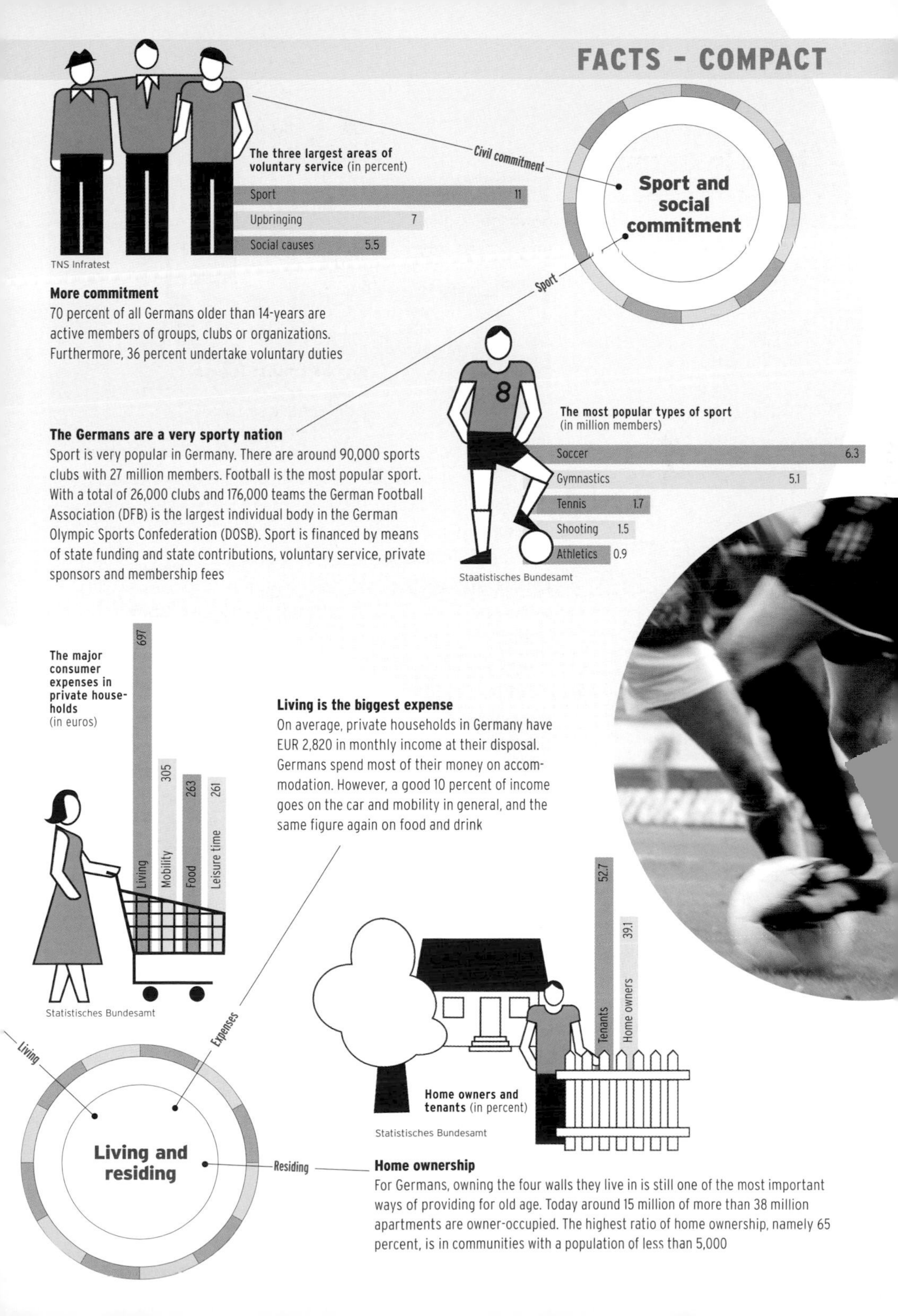

More commitment
70 percent of all Germans older than 14-years are active members of groups, clubs or organizations. Furthermore, 36 percent undertake voluntary duties

The Germans are a very sporty nation
Sport is very popular in Germany. There are around 90,000 sports clubs with 27 million members. Football is the most popular sport. With a total of 26,000 clubs and 176,000 teams the German Football Association (DFB) is the largest individual body in the German Olympic Sports Confederation (DOSB). Sport is financed by means of state funding and state contributions, voluntary service, private sponsors and membership fees

Living is the biggest expense
On average, private households in Germany have EUR 2,820 in monthly income at their disposal. Germans spend most of their money on accommodation. However, a good 10 percent of income goes on the car and mobility in general, and the same figure again on food and drink

Home ownership
For Germans, owning the four walls they live in is still one of the most important ways of providing for old age. Today around 15 million of more than 38 million apartments are owner-occupied. The highest ratio of home ownership, namely 65 percent, is in communities with a population of less than 5,000

Women in the world of work: Women now account for 45 percent of all employed persons

Top jobs
Women account for some 21 percent of leading executives in Germany, and every third manager is a woman. In Eastern Germany, the ratio of female to male managers is far more even. There a good 42 percent of managers are women and as many as 29 percent of the key executives are women. In Western Germany, the figures are only 32 and 20 percent respectively. The opportunities for women to assume management responsibilities depends strongly on the sector. It is highest in the service industry, where 53 percent of managers are women. In the construction industry, by contrast, the figure is only 14 percent.

With regard to wages and salaries there continue to be differences between the sexes: Female workers, for example, earn just 74 percent of their male counterparts' pay, and salaried staff a mere 71 percent. For the most part this is due to the fact that women frequently work in lower positions. Even though nowadays they are frequently getting to occupy **top jobs** on the career ladder, in doing so they still encounter considerable hurdles. As an example, almost 50 percent of students are women but only a third, research assistants, and just 15 percent professors with tenure.

One of the main obstacles to climbing the career ladder is the fact that the network of childcare facilities particularly for small infants is not so good on a European comparison, not to forget that relatively little has changed with regard to the division of domestic labor between men and women. In 75 to 90 percent of all families it is women who do the core of traditional housework. And although 80 percent of fathers would like to spend more time with their children, women, even those in employment, invest twice as much time looking after children as men. To date it was almost exclusively women who have taken parental leave. Yet in the first nine months after introduction of parental support (see p. 151), the proportion of fathers who have taken leave to concentrate on childcare has almost trebled to 9.6 percent, whereby half of the men only want to stay at home for two months.

Women are well established in politics. In the SPD and CDU, the two main parties, almost every third and fourth member respectively is female. The rise in the proportion of women in the Bundestag is nothing if not remarkable. Whereas in 1980 they made up just eight percent of all members of parliament, in 2005 this figure had risen to almost 32 percent. The same year Angela Merkel became the first woman to become German Chancellor.

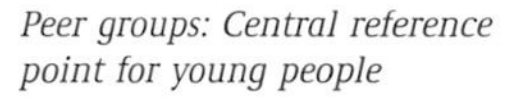

Peer groups: Central reference point for young people

Youth

Alongside their peers of the same age, whose importance has risen appreciably, the main group to which young people relate is the family. Never before have so many youngsters – 73 percent of 18 to 21-year-olds – lived at home for so long. Almost all 12 to 29-year-olds state that they have a very good, trustworthy relationship with their parents.

One reason for staying at home so long is that more and more young people are staying in the education system for longer and longer. Their **standard of qualification** has risen considerably. In total, 43.4 percent of each year-group (18 to 20-year-olds) are entitled to study at a university, and 36 percent of each year-group opt for such study in the medium term. In particular young people from lower social classes

Standard of qualification
Around 60 percent of young people go into vocational training for a state-recognized profession either on the dual vocational training system or as school training in a vocational college. A good 36 percent enroll in one of the 383 universities.

Value priorities among young people

Friends and family increasingly important
Compared with the 1980s, young people in Germany have become decidedly more pragmatic. The young generation focuses on achievement, commitment and goals. Today, the 12-25 year-olds attach great value to friends and family. Given an increasingly sensitive perception of social problems (especially as regards their own career opportunities), they seek security and support. 69 percent are worried that they might lose their jobs or not find adequate employment.

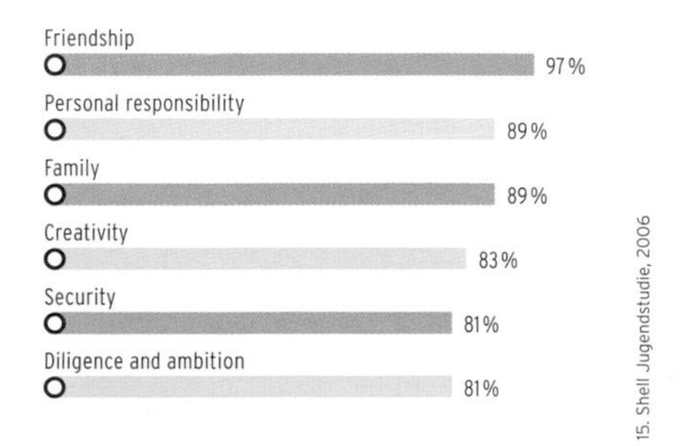

and immigrant families represent problem groups for the education system.

In comparison with earlier generations of young people youngsters have become more pragmatic and not only have a good relationship with their parents' generation but also with democracy: The pessimistic protest and "can't be bothered" attitude of the 1980s has for the most part given way to a non-ideological, optimistic pragmatism. Today's young generation is success-oriented and prepared to work hard. Their maxim of life can be reduced to the formula "getting on instead of getting out".

Social commitment
Social commitment among young people in Germany is gratifyingly high. Indeed, 36 percent of the young people in the 14-24 year age bracket do voluntary work. They are active on behalf of sports, leisure time, school, cultural and church affairs or in the emergency services. The proportion of young people in some areas is so high that without their commitment the services would collapse – for example in the field of sports. Half of all young people are members of clubs, a quarter dedicated to large social organizations, especially to the churches.

With regard to the traditional left-wing/right-wing divide, today's youth is typically positioned somewhat to the left of the population as a whole; only very occasionally are there instances of political extremism. On the other hand there is a high degree of willingness to get involved with **social commitment**. Some three-quarters of all youngsters are actively committed to social and ecological interests: elderly people in need of help, environment and animal protection, the poor, immigrants and the disabled. Interest in politics, political parties and trade unions, on the other hand, is on the decline. Only about 30 percent of 12 to 25-year old youngsters claim to be at all interested in politics, whereas among young adults and students the figure is considerable higher, namely 44 and 64 percent respectively.

Young people: Helping others is a self-evident part of their lives

The elderly

In Germany, approximately every fourth person is over 60 years old. Because of the long-standing low birth rates and increasing life expectancy, after Japan and Italy German society has the third-largest proportion of elderly people worldwide. Their ways of life and **lifestyles** have changed a lot over the last decades. Nowadays the vast majority of elderly people lead independent lives. For the most part they live close to their children, with whom they are in close contact. Health-wise the "young elderly", who are younger than 75 or 80, are mostly in a position to carry on living independent lives with new goals and actively decide how to make use of their leisure time.

Financially speaking the elder generation is for the most part taken care of: The 1957 pensions reform gradually gave pensioners a full share in the nation's wealth. Today it is even possible for them to give their children financial support to start their own family. Poverty in old age has not been done away with entirely, but the risk of being poor in old age is lower than that of other age groups.

Increasingly seldom do families of three generations live under one and the same roof, but there are strong emotional bonds between grown-up children and their parents and between grandparents and grandchildren. A Federal Government specimen project seeks to strengthen cross-generational ties. Thus in coming years each district and municipality in Germany will seek to establish a so-called multi-generational house. To date, 460 such houses are receiving financial support, forming a point of contact, network and hub for family advice, health support, crisis intervention and care planning.

Life style of the elder generations
Senior citizens are not only growing older, but are healthier, fitter and more active than in the past. They are also economically better off: the over-60s hold almost a third of total purchasing power. The life style of the 50+ generation has changed considerably, and the silver-agers increasingly prioritize active leisure time. According to an SWR study, here they emphasize nurturing social contacts. Alongside almost daily viewing TV (news), listening to radio (classic) and reading the paper, they like to do sports.

Immigration and integration

Ever since the 1950s post-war boom the German economy has been dependent on immigrant workers. The majority of those who were at the time referred to as "guest workers"

Foreign population

Immigration
As early as the 19th century Germany attracted a large number of immigrants and since the 1950s has emerged as the European country with the largest immigrant population. In 1950, there were about 500,000 foreigners in Germany, accounting for a mere one percent or so of the population. This has changed emphatically: Today, some 7.3 million foreigners live in Germany, or 8.8 percent of the population, including 2.2 million EU citizens. About every fifth foreigner living in Germany was born here and is a second or third-generation immigrant.

have now returned to their home countries in South and Southeast Europe, but many have stayed on in Germany to earn their keep. Many of the Turkish immigrants who came to Germany at a later date have also remained in the country. This has resulted in Germany gradually developing from a country that accommodated guest workers to a country with regulated immigration.

Repatriates of German descent, who for generations have been living in the states of the former Soviet Union, Romania and Poland, are a second major group of immigrants. Since the collapse of the communist systems they have been returning to Germany in increasing numbers.

These two groups of immigrants resulted in the per capita rate of **immigration** to Germany in the 1980s being considerably higher than that of classic immigration countries such as the USA, Canada and Australia. There are more than seven million foreigners, in other words almost nine percent of the population, living in Germany. In addition there are

Religions

About two thirds of the population in Germany state that they are of the Christian faith. About half of them are Roman Catholics, the other half Protestants. Almost one third do not belong to a religious community, something that can mainly be attributed to reunification and the fact that citizens in the East German states are mainly not members of a particular confession.
In the aftermath of the Nazi genocide, very few persons of the Jewish faith lived in Germany. Today, the Jewish communities have a good 100,000 members. Increasingly, other religions are gaining in importance in Germany, too. For example, many of the foreigners living in Germany are of the Muslim faith. About 3.3 million Muslims from 40 different countries live in Germany, which is why such importance is attached to the dialog with Islam.
The Basic Law guarantees the freedom of religion and to exercise one's faith. There is no state church in Germany, but the state participates, among other things, in financing denominational kindergartens and schools. The churches levy a church tax which the state collects on their behalf: It is used to fund social services such as advisory centers, church kindergartens, schools, hospitals and homes for senior citizens. Religious instruction in schools in Germany is unique in structure: It comes under state supervision, but the churches are responsible for the content.

also 1.5 million foreigners who have taken German citizenship, and some 4.5 million repatriates. In total, around 15 million people in Germany have an "immigrant background" which the German Statistics Office defines, among other things, as including naturalized foreigners as well as children with one foreign parent. Among the foreigners, some 1.7 million persons with Turkish citizenship form the largest group, followed by the Italians with 530,000.

Over the past two decades progress has been made with regard to the integration of immigrants: Acquiring German citizenship has also been facilitated, contacts between immigrants and Germans are closer, and there is more widespread acceptance of ethnic cultural variety. And the new **immigration law** provides for the first time an all-embracing legal framework that considers all aspects of immigration policy. And yet integration remains a challenge for politicians and society alike. The Federal Government considers the integration of foreigners living in Germany to be a focus of its work, and is foregrounding improving language skills, education and integration into the labor market. In July 2006, Federal Chancellor Angela Merkel initiated the first Integration Summit inviting representatives of all social groups impacting on integration to attend. The result was a "National Integration Plan", presented in mid-2007. It contains clear goals as well as over 400 concrete measures for government and non-government actors. Thus, a network of "education patrons" are to support children and young people from immigrant families in their education and training, and the business federations have agreed to offer young migrants better training opportunities. Implementation of the plan is to be monitored on a regular basis. ●

Ethno-cultural diversity: About every sixth inhabitant is an immigrant or a member of a family of immigrants

Immigration law
In early 2005 the first Immigration Act in German history came into force. It distinguishes between limited residence permits and unlimited right of residence. At the same time, it sets out measures to integrate immigrants, such as mandatory language courses.

Rainer Geißler
Professor of Sociology at Siegen University, Geißler is the author of the standard sociology textbook "Die Sozialstruktur Deutschlands".

Social security

AFFLUENCE FOR EVERYBODY AND SOCIAL JUSTICE: In the late 1950s that was the goal the then Federal Minister of Economics Ludwig Erhard had in mind when he introduced the social market economy in Germany. The "German model" proved to be a success story and became an archetype for several other countries. One of the pillars of this success was the extensive German welfare system. Today, Germany boasts one of the most comprehensive welfare systems: 27.6 percent of the country's gross domestic product is channeled into public welfare spending. In comparison, the USA invests 16.2 percent, while the OECD average is 20.7 percent. An all-embracing system of health, pension, accident, long-term care, and **unemployment insurance** provides protection against the financial consequences of the risks we face in everyday life. In addition, the welfare lifeline offers tax-financed services such as the family services equalization scheme (child benefit, tax concessions) or basic provisions for pensioners and those unable to work. Germany sees itself as a **welfare state** that considers the social protection of all its citizens to be a priority.

The welfare-state social systems in Germany have a long tradition dating back to the industrial revolution. In the late 19th century, Reich Chancellor Otto von Bismarck devised the principles of the state social insurance scheme; It was under his aegis that the laws relating to accident and health insurance as well as provisions for invalidity and old age were passed. Whereas in those days a mere ten percent of the population benefited from the welfare legislation, nowadays almost 90 percent of people in Germany enjoy its protection.

In subsequent decades the welfare lifeline was expanded and refined; in 1927, for example, insurance covering the financial consequences of unemployment and, in 1995, **long-term care insurance** were introduced. The 21st century calls for a fundamental structural realignment to the systems, in particular with regard to whether they can be

Unemployment insurance
In Germany those with no work can claim support. Anyone who is unemployed and over the past two years has paid contributions to the state unemployment insurance system for at least 12 months is entitled to unemployment benefit (60 to 67 percent of their last net income). This unemployment benefit is financed through the contributions of which employers and employees each pay half. The longest period for which unemployment benefit can be drawn is six and 24 months. After that period those looking for work can apply for basic support (known as "unemployment benefit II"), which is assessed according to the applicant's needs.

The welfare state
The principle of the welfare state is enshrined in Article 20 of the Basic Law and cannot be rescinded, even if the Basic Law is changed. In this way the Basic Law commits the state to protect, in addition to their freedom, the natural bases of life of its citizens. Each individual, however, also has to assume responsibility for his own social welfare.

financed in the long term: The increasing proportion of elderly people in the population in conjunction with a relatively low birth rate and trends in the labor market have pushed the social security system to its very limits. By means of extensive reforms politicians are now busy attempting to meet this challenge and ensure a welfare system based on solidarity for coming generations as well.

Long-term care insurance
Long-term care insurance was introduced in 1995 as the "fifth pillar" of the social insurance system. The compulsory insurance is financed by equal contributions by employers and employees. There are plans to extend this financing through provisions covered by capital.

Reform of the health system

Germany is one of the countries with the best medical care. A wide range of hospitals, medical practices and institutions guarantees medical care for everybody. With over four million jobs, health care is the largest employment sector in Germany. All in all, 10.7 percent of the country's gross domestic product is spent on health – 1.7 percent more than the average in the OECD member countries. As a result of the so-called cost-cutting law introduced in the wake of the reform

A family-friendly society

In Germany family promotion is playing an increasingly important role and is correspondingly supported by the state. In order to encourage men and women to have more children again, since 2007 the child-raising benefit has been replaced by a means-tested parent's benefit financed through taxes. Thus, for a period of one year one parent who interrupts his or her career to raise children receives 67 percent of their last net income, or a minimum of 300 and a maximum of 1,800 euro. This period is extended to 14 months if the second parent likewise stays at home for at least two months. The aim here is to make it more natural for fathers to take time off to raise children as well. At the same time there are plans to extend child care. Until now every child has had the legal right to a place at kindergarten from the age of three until they start school. By 2013, 750,000 crêche slots are to be set up for the under-3s, thus catering for one third of all children children under 3. This is intended to make it easier for mothers and fathers to combine working and raising a family.
The monthly child benefit is EUR 154 for each child (EUR 179 as of the fourth child) until the age of 18. The legal right to up to three years leave from work also makes an important contribution to supporting young parents. Furthermore, as long as there are no valid company reasons against it, young parents can choose to work part time.

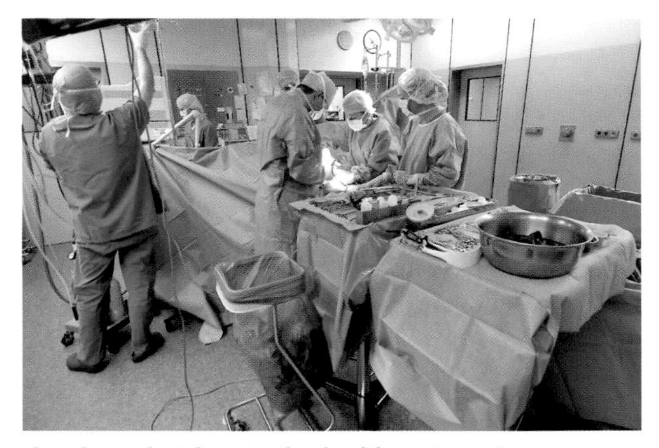

High standards: Germany is one of the countries with the best medical care

Health insurance
Almost all citizens in Germany have health insurance, whether as a compulsory member of the statutory health insurance scheme (88 percent) or a private health insurance scheme (almost 12 percent). The health insurance companies cover the cost of medical treatment, medication, hospitalization and preventive health care. Contributions to the health insurance scheme are made by employees and employers. Non-employed family members of those in a compulsory health insurance scheme do not pay any contributions.

Accident insurance
Statutory accident insurance is a liability insurance on the part of employers in favor of employees who are thereby protected from the consequences of an accident at work or an occupational disease.

already undertaken to the health system, Germany now makes the lowest per capita increase to health spending of all OECD countries: Between 2000 and 2005 spending rose in real terms by 1.3 percent per annum, while the OECD mean was 4.3 percent.

Yet there is still a need for further reform. To this end, 2007 saw the government resolve the reform of the health-care system. The key pillar to the reform is the introduction of a Health Fund: From 2009 onwards, insured persons' contributions to the statutory **health insurance** companies will be standardized. For each insured person, the health insurance companies will receive a flat rate from the Health Fund. At the same time, tax financing of health insurance services

The topic on the Internet

www.bmfsfj.de
The Federal Ministry for Family Affairs, Senior Citizens, Women and Young People offers information on state support as well as the wording of laws (German)

www.shell-jugendstudie.de
With support from the Shell corporation, for five decades now, scientists and research institutions have been studying the values and life of young people (German)

www.bmg.bund.de
On its Web site the Federal Ministry of Health makes available news, data, background information, and links to further sources relating to health (English, French, German, Italian, Spanish, Turkish)

www.deutsche-sozialversicherung.de
The Web site run by the European representative agency of the leading umbrella organizations in the German social insurance system provides information on social insurance in Germany with countless links (English, French, German)

will commence, such as contribution-exempt insuring of the children of insured parents, with an annual increment in the support provided by the government – up to a grand total of EUR 14 billion. From 2009 onwards, there will also be compulsory insurance for everyone: The private health insurance companies will be obliged to accept insured persons at a base rate.

Pension reform

Fundamental changes have also been made to provisions for old age. Although compulsory **pension insurance** will remain the single most important pillar of income in old age, in-company and private pension schemes are becoming more and more important. The so-called "Riester pension" and the "Rürup pension" for the self-employed are models already in existence enabling by means of tax concessions private pension schemes covered by capital contributions. Part of the reform involves raising the mandatory retirement age from 65 to 67: Between 2012 and 2035 the initial retirement age will rise by one month a year, while the "Initiative 50 Plus" will enhance job prospects for older employees.

Further reforms

The reform of support for the long-term unemployed and those receiving **social assistance** has already been implemented. With the introduction of basic support for the unemployed those who had formerly been receiving social security, as long as they were capable of working, were put on a par with the long-term unemployed. The reform of the **accident insurance** scheme, aimed primarily at reforming the organizational framework, is still outstanding. ●

Pension insurance
The statutory pension insurance is the most important pillar of old-age provisions. Its financing is split: The monthly contributions paid by employees and employers pay the pensions of those currently in retirement. Through their contributions, those insured acquire some rights when they themselves become pensioners. In turn, coming generations provide for these future rents with their contributions (cross-generational contract). In addition, company and private pensions are the second and third pillars of provisions for old age. Under certain conditions these also enjoy government support.

Social assistance
Another feature of the social lifeline is social assistance, which is financed through taxes. It comes into effect when people are unable to escape their plight on their own and by their own means or by those of relatives. There is also basic support like social assistance, such as basic protection in old age or in the case of long-term unemployment as well as state help towards living or to assist persons in certain predicaments.

10

Culture

There are many sides to cultural life in Germany: From North to South there are around 300 theaters and 130 professional orchestras. The museum world is of quite unparalleled quality - featuring 500 art museums with diverse internationally renowned collections. Young German painting is equally vibrant, and is long since part of the international scene. And Germany is one of the major book nations, with around 95,000 new books and re-editions each year. The 350 dailies and thousands of magazines go to show how lively the German media world is. Moreover, German films are once again a great success at home and abroad.

Berlinale Palast

For the True, Beautiful and Good – the German cultural world

LAND OF THE POETS AND THINKERS. Goethe was German, as were Beethoven and Bach. And yet this land of culture still has no national authority with overall responsibility for culture for the country as a whole. According to the Basic Law, culture is the responsibility of the individual federal states. These see themselves as the guardians and supporters of **cultural federalism** in Germany. Why is it that cultural affairs in Germany are something that the nation itself as a whole cannot, or is not meant to, govern? Ever since the era of Kaiser Wilhelm II in the late 19th century, German culture as the expression of a single German nation was suspected of being the reflection of a craving for status. The disaster of National Socialism ultimately resulted in a re-alignment. Following the Second World War the opinion gradually gained sway that Germany would only be able to return to the world community if it avoided all semblance of exaggerated emotionalism as regards the national culture, which in turn led to a rejection of any form of national cultural policy in Germany.

Yet in Germany cultural institutions are more widely spread than in most other countries. Cultural federalism kindles the ambitions of the individual federal states. Cultural policy is local policy. The state of Baden-Württemberg uses culture as a "soft factor" in its promotional activities. Film promotion has also become an instrument of federal government. Money flows from wherever films are produced. Since the late 1990s the Ruhr region, the mining and steelworking district in North Rhine-Westphalia, has been re-inventing itself as a successful cultural region. Only since

Conducting the Berlin Philharmonic: Sir Simon Rattle

Cultural federalism
Given its federal structure, in Germany culture is the core area where the 16 states possess sovereignty. The Basic Law accords the Federal Government few powers on cultural questions, and thus most cultural institutions are maintained by the states and municipalities. This independent cultural life in the states has led to cultural centers arising all over the country. There are world-class cultural offerings to be found even in smaller cities. The German Cultural Council functions at the national level as the politically independent working party of the Federal cultural associations and discusses cross-disciplinary matters of cultural policy.

State Minister for Culture and Media
Since in Germany culture comes under the ambit of the states, there is no federal ministry of culture. A State Minister for Culture coordinates activities in the field of cultural policy.

German Federal Cultural Foundation
The German Federal Cultural Foundation was established in 2002 and acts nationally and internationally. By supporting relevant projects, it focuses primarily on the challenges of art and culture in the 21st century. The German Federal Cultural Foundation is based in Halle an der Saale.

1998 has a **State Minister for Culture and Media** been part of the Federal Chancellery in Berlin. Since then Germany has once again seen this or that cultural matter as being something the entire country should be involved with.

Federal film production was re-organized, and the **German Federal Cultural Foundation** founded. Berlin is increasingly turning into a cultural magnet and has already become a unique cultural force, a melting pot of cultures, whose museums are a reflection of the entire history of humanity. The Holocaust Memorial in the heart of the city is testimony hewn in stone to how Germany as a cultural nation is dealing with its history. It is impressive proof of a form of national cultural policy that has become necessary since the dawn of the new century. Cultural federalism can likewise be maintained; it continues to act as guarantor for a highly diverse, sophisticated cultural scene in Germany.

Literature

New story-tellers: Daniel Kehlmann and Julia Franck ("Die Mittagsfrau"), winner of the German Book Prize 2007

Germany is a book country: With around 95,000 titles published or re-published annually, it is one of the world's leading book nations. The licenses for almost 9,000 German books are sold to foreign companies annually. In the fall of each year, the publishing world gathers in Germany at the world's largest meeting of the trade, the **International Frankfurt Book Fair**. Held each spring, the Leipzig Book Fair is a smaller event that has now become well established.

Despite the Internet and TV, Germans still love to read. A lot of water has recently passed under the literary bridge. Although the generation of leading post-war German authors such as Hans Magnus Enzensberger, Siegfried Lenz, Christa Wolf and Literature Nobel Prize winner Günter Grass is still revered, nonetheless, at the beginning of the 21st century their work no longer stands for aesthetic innovation.

Whereas after the Second World War there was a quest for moral answers and, following on from 1968, a preponderance of social analyses, the years following the fall of the Wall were defined by mass culture, whereby even minor

Literary buffs from the world over meet at Frankfurt's International Book Fair

events became major, and authors turned into pop stars you could actually meet. And today? What is the dominant force in the German **book market**? Writers such as Sten Nadolny, Uwe Timm, F. C. Delius, Brigitte Kronauer and Ralf Rothmann, who emerged before the 1990s, honor the continuation of high-quality narrative traditions. The anguish of present-day life, art as a last refuge for self-assertion: Botho Strauss is moving in this direction.

While the literature of the younger generation was less intensively read in the 1980s and 1990s, with the exception of Patrick Süskind's international bestseller "Perfume" and Bernhard Schlink's "The Reader", since the beginning of the new millennium things have changed noticeably. Today, there is a new thirst to tell stories, with authors such as Daniel Kehlmann, Thomas Brussig, Katharina Hacker, Julia Franck and Ilja Trojanow also captivating German readers, who are now dedicated to German literature almost more than ever before. Clear proof of this are the number of copies published of Kehlmann's "Measuring the World", a novel which in 2006 was one of the world's best-selling books, and Trojanow's "Der Weltensammler". As regards books for children and young people, one of the most successful authors is Cornelia Funke ("Inkheart"). The German Book Prize ensures the winners greater national and international exposure.

What is striking is that the former lines dividing highbrow literature and entertaining works are becoming blurred. The in-label in the review pages is "new legibility. Gone are the days of a close link between politics and literature. Dreams of revolt and obstinacy still abound. What

Book market
Books and the culture of reading continue to be held in high regard in Germany. In 2006, the German book market generated sales estimated at some EUR 9.3 billion. The entire output of items produced for the book trade by German publishers comes to around 970 million books and similar printed matter. In Germany there are more than 4,000 book stores and 7,500 libraries, with the major publishing cities being Munich, Berlin, Frankfurt/Main, Stuttgart, Cologne and Hamburg.

International Frankfurt Book Fair
The International Frankfurt Book Fair has taken place every autumn since 1949 and is the outstanding annual international book trade get-together. The highpoint of every book fair is the award-giving ceremony for the Peace Prize of the German Book Trade, which has been won by the likes of Václav Havel, Jorge Semprún and Susan Sontag. Since 2005, to mark the beginning of the Book Fair, the German Book Prize is presented for the best novel written in German.

Leading the way – yesterday and today

Celebrated classics, courageous visionaries:
The history of German art and culture is rich in men and women renowned for extraordinary achievements. Many are household names outside the country, too

Johann Sebastian Bach
Virtuoso Baroque church music: Johann Sebastian Bach (1685-1750) perfected the stringent "art of the fugue", writing more than 200 cantata and oratories

Friedrich von Schiller
Champion of liberty: Theater was the passion of Friedrich von Schiller (1759-1805). The author of "The Robbers" and "Wilhelm Tell" was one of the first to put politics on stage

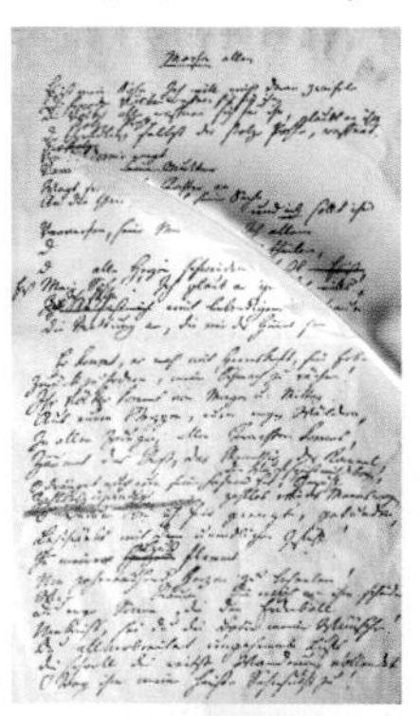

Johann Wolfgang von Goethe
Poet, playwright, scholar: Johann Wolfgang von Goethe (1749-1832) is regarded as the "all-round genius" and the classic of German literature

Ludwig van Beethoven
Pioneer of Romanticism: Ludwig van Beethoven (1770-1827) focused full on form while bringing a completely new measure of personal expression and sensibility to bear in music

Literature
Literature
Music
Music
15th – 20th century
Literature
Visual Arts
Visual Arts

Joseph Beuys
Inventor of the "expanded concept of art": "Every person is an artist" was his most famous saying. Joseph Beuys (1921-1986) caused a real stir with his spectacular Action and Environment art

Thomas Mann
Master of the novel and the novella: Thomas Mann (1875-1955) won the Nobel Prize for Literature for his family epic "Buddenbrooks"

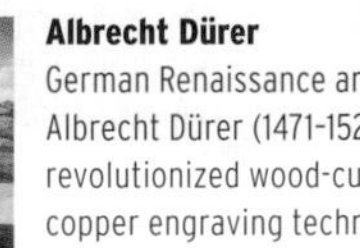

Albrecht Dürer
German Renaissance artist: Albrecht Dürer (1471-1528) revolutionized wood-cutting and copper engraving techniques

Anne-Sophie Mutter
The violin virtuoso: Anne-Sophie Mutter, born in 1963, is a star of classical music celebrated the world over. She was supported from an early age by conductor Herbert von Karajan and is highly regarded as a Mozart expert

Wim Wenders
The master of the silent image: Multiple award-winning director, born in 1945, made "Paris, Texas" and "Wings of Desire"

Pina Bausch
Creator of modern dance theater: Pina Bausch, born in 1940, invented a new body language for dance

Music

Film

Ballet

Music

21st century

Literature

Visual Arts

Photography

Karlheinz Stockhausen
Composer of serial and electronic music: Karlheinz Stockhausen (1928 – 2007), is one of the major contemporary composers

Günter Grass
Author of "The Tin Drum": Literature Nobel Prize Winner Günter Grass, born in 1927, is unparalleled in his ability to turn history into literature. In 2006 it became known that as a 17-year-old he was a member of the "Waffen-SS".

Gerhard Richter
Of all living artists, his works are the most expensive: Gerhard Richter, born in 1932, constantly surprises us with new techniques and topics, his breadth ranges from photorealism to abstract art

Bernd and Hilla Becher
Photographers as Concept artists: With their architectural photographs the couple has created an artistic form of documentation and strongly influenced the younger generation of German photo artists

Authors
Young authors with immigrant roots contribute new themes and stimuli to German language and literature. They include Ilja Trojanow, Wladimir Kaminer, Sasa Stanisic, Terézia Mora or Feridun Zaimoglu.

counts, however, is authenticity. The functions have shifted and perceptions changed because there is a lack not only of **authors** producing ambitious literature for society, but also of readers that wish to read it.

Theater

Theater world
With 120 public theaters with more than 750 stages and 185 private theaters, Germany is a theater giant. The best-known venues include Thalia Theater in Hamburg, the Berlin Ensemble and Munich's Kammerspiele.

Outside the country, German theater frequently has a reputation for being brash and self-absorbed. It is, however, theater with a system behind it that is admired the world over. Even small towns boast opera houses and ballet troupes as well as theaters; overall there is a distinct **theater world**, a well-established network of state, municipal, traveling, and private theaters. As the student revolts of 1968 died down a broad-ranged **theater scene** also emerged: the fringe groups – who even today are the symbol of an uninterrupted passion for theater that wants to take the limelight. In Germany a lot goes into this system: in terms of stimulus, attention and money. For many this

Foreign Cultural Policy

Alongside classical diplomacy and foreign economic policy, foreign cultural and education policy is the third pillar of German foreign policy. The goal: to provide a up-to-date image of Germany in the European integration process and to participate in fostering mutual understanding between peoples. The German Federal Foreign Office only implements part of the cultural policy, tending instead to commission intermediary agencies such as the Goethe-Institut or the Institut für Auslandsbeziehungen (ifa). The Goethe-Institut runs 147 cultural institutions in 83 countries, 13 of them in Germany. They offer German lessons, assist foreign teachers of German, organize readings, theater and film events, and discussions. ifa is primarily engaged in cultural dialog. Since 2003, in cooperation with the Federal Foreign Office and non-profit foundations it has financed cultural centers above all in the Middle and Eastern Europe. German schools abroad are also of great importance. There are 117 of them, with a total of 70,000 pupils (53,000 are not German nationals). With the "Schools: Partners of the Future", the Federal Foreign Office is specifically supporting school work abroad. Here, for example, a network of partner schools is to be established in which German is taught as a foreign language. Following the terrorist attacks of Sept. 11, 2001 the Federal Foreign Office launched a special program entitled "European-Islamic Cultural Dialog" to help improve mutual understanding.
www.goethe.de, www.daad.de, www.avh.de, www.ifa.de, www.auslandsschulwesen.de

Wuppertal dance theater: The Pina Bausch ensemble is famous worldwide

is a luxury, especially as box office takings amount to a mere 10–15 percent of theater expenses. Private theaters are also included in the public system of subsidization – for example the famous Berliner Schaubühne, which was founded and heavily influenced by renowned director Peter Stein. Admittedly the system has long since reached its zenith and is now in a difficult position because time and again art is measured in terms of the material requirements.

For a long time Peter Stein was considered to be a unique figure in German theater. As opposed to other directors he created an oeuvre that is clearly recognizable by virtue of the continuity of repeated motifs, themes and authors. A theater of memory, with a directing style that takes its cue from the text. There are worlds between today's up-and-coming generation of dramatists and a Peter Stein, Peter Zadek and Claus Peymann, the head of the Berliner Ensemble. Contemporary theater can no longer be portrayed using the vocabulary of the 1968 rebels. Terms such as enlighten, instruct, expose, and intervene sound antiquated. The theater of today's young people no longer sees itself as being avant-garde; it strives for independent forms of expression.

Following the euphoria with youth of the 1990s, when names such as Leander Haußmann, Stefan Bachmann and Thomas Ostermeier grabbed the headlines, a phase has emerged in which directors such as these have become theater managers.

Theater scene
German theater is considered one of the most experimental world-wide. German companies have set the standard not least as regards dance theater. One of the key protagonists of modern dance is Pina Bausch, acclaimed as the major female choreographer of the day. Another international dance theater star is Sasha Waltz – born in Karlsruhe she is a choreographer and dancer at the Berliner Schaubühne.

Creative industry
Imagination and creativity are a key factor driving the German economy. Art, film, music, fashion, media and lifestyle: Accounting for 800,000 jobs and gross value added of EUR 35 billion, in Germany this dynamic sector places between the chemicals and power industries, and generates a key proportion of gross domestic product.

The Schaubühne in Berlin: In the late 1960s it saw the radical revival of German theater under directors such as Peter Stein, Luc Bondy and Klaus-Michael Grüber

The Berliner Ensemble am Schiffbauerdamm: Once Bertolt Brecht was active here, today it is the domain of star international directors such as Robert Wilson

Together with his Berliner Volksbühne, Frank Castorf, well known for taking plays apart, and dismantling and putting text together again, has become a role model for this new generation of dramatists. Christoph Marthaler and Christoph Schlingensief also represent a different interpretation of what theater is about, namely a platform that responds to the displacements following the end of the Cold War and the emergence of global capitalism. Directors such as Michael Thalheimer, Armin Petras, Martin Kusej, René Pollesch and Christina Paulhofer have created styles of directing that prioritize style over content; traditional narrative methods that stick close to the text are not something they are necessarily familiar with. What determined German theater for some 250 years, the confrontation with society, has given way to colorful variety, as is demonstrated by the annual **Berliner Theatertreffen**. Theater, however, has never ignored the era in which it is played. It has to create images of our life. And it is remembrance work. This is why theater is subsidized: for this very public function.

Berliner Theatertreffen
Berliner Theatertreffen is organized by the Berlin Festival and is the single most important German theater festival. Held each year since 1964 in May, it showcases the ten "most striking productions" of the season, selected by a jury of theater critics from around 400 performances. In addition, the Theatertreffen provides a platform for young playwrights to present their new work at a "script shop".

Music

Germany's reputation as a musical nation is still based on names like Bach, Beethoven, Brahms, Handel and Richard Strauss. Students from around the world flock to its music academies, music lovers attend the **festivals** – from the Wagner Festival in Bayreuth to the Donaueschingen Festival of Contemporary Music. There are 80 publicly financed concert halls in Germany, the most important being in Hamburg, Berlin, Dresden and Munich as well as Frankfurt/Main and Leipzig. In recent times in the race for the annual critics' "Opera House of the Year" prize it was Stuttgart that most frequently came out on top. The Berlin Philharmonic, under the star British conductor Sir Simon Rattle, is considered to be the best of around 130 symphony **orchestras** in Germany. The Frankfurt "Ensemble Modern" is a fundamental engine room behind contemporary music production. Every year it masters some 70 new works, including 20 premieres. In addition to maestros such as Kurt Masur and Christoph Eschenbach, of the young conductors Ingo Metzmacher and Christian Thielemann in particular have come to the fore. Of the artists, the soprano Waltraud Meier, baritone Thomas Quasthoff and clarinetist Sabine Meyer are among the best in the world. The violinist Anne-Sophie Mutter even has an enormous following beyond classical music enthusiasts.

Karlheinz Stockhausen, the pioneer of electronic music and his traditionalist opposite number, opera composer Hans Werner Henze, have had a resounding influence on contemporary music since the 1950s. Nowadays there are a wide array of stylistic trends: Heiner Goebbels combines music and theater, while Helmut Lachenmann takes the possibilities of instrumental expression to the extreme. Wolfgang Rihm reveals how in the way it is developing it appears possible for music once again to become more comprehensible. On the other end of the musical spectrum, pop singers such as Herbert Grönemeyer have been enjoying success with songs in German for years now, as have the Punk rock band "Die Toten Hosen", the Hip-Hop group "Die Fantastischen Vier" and "Tokio Hotel". Furthermore, over the past few years young artists such as the singer Xavier Naidoo (of the group "Söhne Mannheims") have been successfully basing their work on American soul and rap. Most recently, the

Festivals
Alongside festivals for classical music, contemporary music is well represented in Germany: with more than 100 special festivals, concert series and studio productions by the opera houses. The Donaueschinger Musiktage are seen as the world's single most important contemporary music festival. The latest developments in music theater are presented at the Biennial in Munich, and the International Music Institute in Darmstadt with its famous "Holiday courses" stands for debate on cutting-edge developments in music.

Orchestras
There are around 130 German professional orchestras, first and foremost among them the Berlin-Philharmonic under Sir Simon Rattle, the Berlin Staatskapelle under Daniel Barenboim, the Gewandhausorchester under Riccardo Chailly, the Bamberg Symphonic under Jonathan Nott and the Munich Philharmonic under Christian Thielemann.

Christian Thielemann: General Musical Director of the Munich Philharmonic

German bands
The most successful exports by German Pop and Rock bands include: Scooter, Seeed, Nena, Kraftwerk, Rammstein, Tokio Hotel, Juli and Mia.

German cinema
German national film productions have clearly picked up at the box offices of late. And there are now once again magnetic stars pulling the crowds into the movie theaters: Alexandra Maria Lara, Martina Gedeck, Julia Jentsch, Daniel Brühl and Moritz Bleibtreu. The industry's greater self-confidence is reflected in the German Film Academy, founded in 2003, which now awards German Oscars once a year: the Lolas. New German films have also scored successes internationally: The second Oscar in five years for a German production went in 2007 to Florian Henckel von Donnersmarck for "The Life of Others". In 2007, Fatih Akin won the prize for best filmscript at the International Film Festival in Cannes and the European Parliament's LUX film prize for his film "The Edge of Heaven".

Berlin band "Wir sind Helden", with lead singer Judith Holofernes

success of the Berlin band "Wir sind Helden" has influenced a whole new wave of young **German bands**. The founding of the "Pop Academy" in Mannheim clearly demonstrated the wish to put German pop music on an international footing.

Cinema

Shortly before the dawn of the new millennium a firework woke the slumbering German film industry: Tom Tykwer's 1998 film "Run Lola Run". The experimental comedy about the redhead Lola, fate, love and chance captures the spirit of the late 1990s. The global audience saw Lola's daredevil race against time through the streets of Berlin as a metaphor for the restlessness of an era. "Run Lola Run" proved to be an international breakthrough for director Tom Tykwer and Franka Potente, who played the leading role.

For the **German cinema** it marked the beginning of a revival. For the first time since the era of the great Rainer Werner Fassbinder (died 1982), foreign commentators once again began to enthuse about German cinema, which is now enjoying international success. In 2002, Caroline Link won an Oscar for "Nowhere in Africa" and in 2007 Florian Henckel von Donnersmarck won the cherished trophy for his film "The Life of Others", and the same year the Cannes International Film Festival awarded its prize for best script and its special prize to Fatih Akin for his film "The Edge of Heaven". In 2007, Tom Tykwer's film of Patrick Süskind's best-selling novel "Perfume" won the German Film Prize in six different categories.

While at the beginning of the new millennium it was comedies that surprisingly boosted German movies' prospects – such as Hans Weingarten's "Die fetten Jahre sind vorbei" (2004) – by the end of the first decade attention focused on serious films. The themes have remained the same, however: The tragicomedy "Good Bye, Lenin!" (Wolfgang Becker, 2003) was a success in almost 70 countries because it portrayed the failure of socialism, and Donnersmarck's "The Life of

Others" (2007) tells the story of life and suffering in East Germany's police state. German films are successes because they use national themes when telling universal stories. And the filmmakers filter the stuff of which their movies are made from the history and difficulties in their own country.

Fatih Akin, a Hamburg citizen with Turkish roots, tells the story of life in Germany at breathtaking speed. In his prize-winning movie "Head-On" (2004), which among others won the B.I.F.F, Golden Bear, he offers us the love story of two Turks brought up in Germany, and how they are crushed between the two cultures. The story is brutally precise, but deliberately not a tear-jerker. And in 2007 in his "Edge of Heaven" Akin tells the story of six people in Germany and Turkey, whose lives are tied up by destiny.

The Gold "Lola" in 2007 went to the jailhouse drama "Vier Minuten" by Chris Kraus. And Monica Bleib-

Director Florian Henckel von Donnersmarck with the Oscar for his film "The Life of Others"

Berlin International Film Festival

Ever since 1951, the Berlin International Film Festival has been held every February. Following the Cannes festival, that in Berlin is the second largest film festival in the world and "the" showcase for German film. For two weeks art, glamour, parties and business all interweave in the heart of Berlin, centering on Potsdamer Platz. Each year, some 430,000 filmgoers and 19,000 trade visitors attend – film stars, film producers, distributors, buyers, financers and journalists. Each Berlin Film Festival climaxes with the international jury awarding the "Bears", the main prizes. With their world or European premieres in Berlin, films from all around the globe vie for the awards.
Alongside the competition, the Berlin Film Festival also features a fest of children's films, a forum for German film, and an international forum for young film. Moreover, the festival includes both a retrospective and an homage to the oeuvre of an outstanding person in film. All in all, each year about 400 films are screened. The federal government contributes EUR 7 million and thus about 40 percent of the total budget, with the rest is raised from entrance tickets and sponsors. Since 2003, each year around 350 young film talents from all over the world are invited to attend the Berlin Film Festival Talent Campus where they acquire new insights and can swap ideas. Dieter Kosslick (photo) is director of the Berlin Film Festival. **www.berlinale.de**

German Film Prize
The German Film Prize takes pride of place among federal cultural support for film. It has been bestowed ever since 1951 for outstanding achievement in German film. In 2007, Tom Tykwer's film version of Patrick Süskind's best-selling novel "Perfume" bagged a total of six awards in different categories.

treu received the German Film Prize for the best lead actress for her role in this dramatic tale of two women and a piano. The renaissance of German film has a strong footing. So the prospects for the German film industry are great.

Fine Arts

Since the 1990s German painting and photography have been enjoying international success. Abroad, this new German painting revelation is known under the label "Young German Artists". The artists involved come from Leipzig, Berlin and Dresden. Neo Rauch is the best known representative of the "New Leipzig School". His style is characterized by a new realism that has emerged, free of all ideology, from the former "Leipzig School" of East German art. The paintings reveal for the most part pale figures that would appear to be waiting for something indefinite; a reflection, perhaps, of the situation in Germany at the beginning of the new millennium. So-called "Dresden Pop", propagated among others by Thomas Scheibitz, references the aesthetics of advertising, TV and video to playfully deal with the aesthetics of finding certainty in the here and now.

Art scene
Older-generation major international artists include among others painters Gerhard Richter, Georg Baselitz, A. R. Penck, Jörg Immendorff, Anselm Kiefer, Markus Lüpertz and Sigmar Polke. Then there are sculptors Ulrich Rückriem and Jochen Gerz as well as performance artist Rebecca Horn - all prime examples of contemporary German art.

For most young artists, dealing with the Nazi era, as was the case in the works of Hans Haacke, Anselm Kiefer and Joseph Beuys, belongs to the past. Rather, a "new interiority" and an interest in spheres of experience that collide with one another are emerging in the **art scene**: The works of Jonathan Meese and André Butzer reflect depression and compulsive phenomena; they are seen as representatives of "Neurotic Realism". The subject of Franz Ackermann's "Mental Maps", in which he points out the disasters behind the facades, is the world as a global village. Tino Seghal, whose art exists only at the time it is performed and is not allowed to be filmed, is aiming for forms of production and communication that have

Neo Rauch Number 1 "Young German Artist"

nothing to do with the market economy. The interest shown in art in Germany can be witnessed at the **documenta**, the leading exhibition of contemporary art worldwide held every five years in Kassel.

As opposed to the Fine Arts – whose importance is underlined by the boom in the foundation of new private museums – photography in Germany had to struggle for a long time to be accepted as an art form in its own right. Katharina Sieverding, who in her self portraits sounds out the boundaries between the individual and society, is considered to be a 1970s pioneer.

The breakthrough came in the 1990s with the success of three young men who studied at the Düsseldorf Academy of Art under photographer duo Bernd and Hilla Becher: Thomas Struth, Andreas Gursky and Thomas Ruff portray in their pictures a double-edged high-gloss reality and possess such a trailblazing influence that internationally they are simply referred to as "Struffsky".

documenta
The documenta in Kassel is the world's most important contemporary art exhibition. Founded on the initiative of painter Arnold Bode, it was first held in 1955, and then every five years for 100 days. The show was swiftly a world success, and will take place for the 13th time in 2012.

Authors
The Kulturzeit editorial desk at 3sat: Dr. Eva Hassel-von Pock, Armin Conrad, Dr. Gudula Moritz, Dr. Rainer M. Schaper, Dr. Monika Sandhack and Stefan Müller (not present).

Art fairs and cultural events

Art Cologne
Art Cologne is the world's oldest art fair and the most important one in Germany

Frankfurt Book Fair
The Frankfurt Book Fair is the world's no. 1 book event

ART COLOGNE

FRANKFURTER BUCHMESSE

BAYREUTHER FESTSPIELE

Berlin Film Festival
The Berlin Film Festival places second to Cannes in the world film event rankings

Leipzig Book Fair
Despite strong competition, the Leipzig Book Fair has established a great reputation for itself

Bayreuth Festival
The Bayreuth Festival on the "green hill" is the event par excellence for "Wagner" enthusiasts

There are some 60,000 full-time journalists in Germany; in Berlin alone almost 1,300 accredited correspondents rub shoulders at the Foreign Press Club or the Government Press Conference

Freedom of the press and speech
In Germany, freedom of communication also means that public agencies are obliged to provide journalists with information. The rights of the press are encoded in the press laws of the federal states. These include the duty to publish an imprint, journalists' duty to take due care in their research and their right to refuse to stand witness or disclose sources. The German Press Council is the voluntary journalism and publishing watchdog: it monitors violations of the duty to take due care in research and of the ethical sides to stories.

Media

By Jo Groebel

GERMANY IS CONSIDERED TO BE A COUNTRY OF books, of deep thought, and of highbrow media. However, Germany has also become a country of DJs and daily soaps. In popular German culture music and TV series, blockbusters in the cinema and the tabloid press are just as important as in other countries – and as the highbrow culture of the poets, the theater and the opera.

Naturally enough there are also some characteristics that are peculiar to the media scene in Germany. These include the emphasis on federal sovereignty in cultural affairs and broadcasting and the dual existence of public and private media, something that cannot be taken for granted in other countries. As regards freedom of the press and speech, in international terms Germany comes off very well. There is pluralism with regard to opinion and information. The press is not in the hands of the government or political parties, but rather in that of societal players. For more than fifty years now the **freedom of the press and speech** has been the common property of everyone and protected by the Constitution. Article 5 of the Basic Law expresses how the Constitution interprets the freedom of the press: "Every person shall have the right freely to express and disseminate his opinions in speech, writing and pictures and to inform himself without hindrance from generally accessible sources. (...) There shall be no censorship."

In general the structure of the German media can be explained by the specific conditions of recent German history. On the one hand the country has experienced extraordinarily troubled times over the past centuries. Many of the theories behind changes in society emerged in Germany or actually took place there. The Enlightenment, Communism, Modernism: All these upheavals, at intervals of less than 30 years – Democratization, the First World War, the Weimar Republic, the Third Reich and Second World War, the East-West conflict and the Cold War, the student revolts and reunification always had a media side to them, indeed

Popular print products: In terms of newspapers density (no. per 1,000 inhabitants), at 298 copies Germany is in the upper middle of the European league tables. Germans spend an average 28 minutes a day reading the paper

would have been unimaginable without the mass media that had emerged in the 19th century. The idea of freedom of opinion and equal rights was disseminated through books and the daily press.

Media usage by hour
Germans use the various media 10 hours a day. First and foremost: radio and TV

Radio	**221 min.**
TV	**220 min.**
Internet	**44 min.**
Newspapers	**28 min.**
Books	**25 min.**
Magazines	**12 min.**

The press

In addition to books, for some 500 years now newspapers and magazines have been a medium that as regards content, form and dissemination may well have been constantly modernized, but whose basic structure has remained more or less the same, despite the continued emergence of new media. Now, as ever, the press stands for in-depth analysis and background reporting, addressing specific topics, and comment. The partial dissolving of fixed ideological convictions in German society along the traditional spectrum of left and right was accompanied in part by the disappearance of a clear cut political allegiance on the part of the press. The German newspaper market is characterized by a large number of publications and regional differences. Alongside 333 regional daily newspapers there are ten national dailies, alongside ten quality publications and nine so-called popular newspapers that concentrate on general interest matters. In this category the influential "Bild"-Zeitung, which is published by Axel Springer Verlag and has a circulation of 3.6 million, is the only national newspaper

The largest German news agency is Deutsche Presse-Agentur (dpa). It ranks 4th worldwide after Reuters, French agency AFP and Associated Press (AP)

Media concentration
Despite the diversity of titles and products, the number of independent publishing houses has steadily dwindled since the mid-1950s. The leading publishers in terms of business muscle and technology have squeezed out competitors in various regional markets. Economic trends in the press market have led to the emergence of large publishing corporations. As regards daily newspapers, it is above all Axel Springer Verlag, which holds a share of some 40 percent of the advertising market for newspapers.

to play an outstanding role. Overall the total circulation figures for some 350 German daily newspapers come to 24 million.

However, the financial footing of the classic daily press is under pressure: The younger generation is reading fewer newspapers, advertising revenue is declining, and all manner of content is nowadays procured from the Internet, which among almost all age groups has now advanced to become a leading medium. Almost two thirds of all Germans are meanwhile “online” – or 48.7 million people over ten years. Nevertheless there is one sold newspaper for more than every third German, and the number of readers is even higher. In terms of politics and culture several publications are considered to be highly influential, for example national quality newspapers such as “Frankfurter Allgemeine Zeitung“, “Süddeutsche Zeitung“ and the traditional weekly “Die Zeit“.

An increasing number of special interest publications have been appearing alongside the popular magazines. The entire range of popular magazines includes some 2,300 publications and boasts a total circulation of more than 120 million. “Stern“, “Focus“ and “Spiegel“, news magazines that play an active role in discussion in society or have

How Germans use the media

The major quality papers

The “Süddeutsche” and the “F.A.Z.” are the German dailies most frequently read (by copies sold)

Newspaper	Copies sold
Süddeutsche Zeitung	431,421
Frankfurter Allgemeine Zeitung	360,915
Die Welt	275,399
Frankfurter Rundschau	152,166
Handelsblatt	143,415
Financial Times Deutschland	103,489

III/2007

The most popular current general interest magazines

In Germany, about 2,300 mass-market magazines and 3,600 trade journals are published

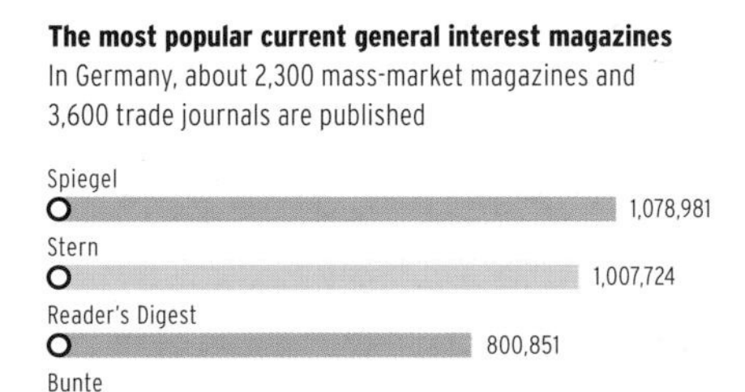

Magazine	Copies
Spiegel	1,078,981
Stern	1,007,724
Reader's Digest	800,851
Bunte	756,472
Focus	728,104
Super Illu	481,455

III/2007

IVW, VDZ, AGF/GfK Fernsehforschung, Denic

themselves been the subject of important discourse, are among the most widely-read publications. Of these, "Spiegel", a political journal with perhaps the greatest long-term influence of any weekly publication, is outstanding. The biggest publishers of popular magazines are Heinrich Bauer Verlag, Axel Springer Verlag, Burda and Gruner+Jahr, which is part of the Bertelsmann Group. Springer and Bertelsmann are also the two media corporations that by virtue of owning successful radio and TV stations, as well as Internet activities, generate sales in the billions, triggering a discussion about **media concentration** and the trans-media concentration of opinion.

Market leader Deutsche Telekom has 16.6 million Web clients. In Germany, at the end of 2007 more than half of all households had a high-speed broadband Internet connection.

Internet and user-generated content

As in most other countries, the German media world faces fundamental challenges by the Internet and mobile communications. First, technically speaking so-called convergence is now a reality, meaning one device or platform unifies telephony, Internet access, video, music and TV. Second, the lines between customized communication for the individual and mass communications thus get obscured.

Popular Web sites

The most frequently visited Internet pages with editorial content in Germany include Spiegel Online, bild.de, and Kicker Online (measured in terms of IVW-certified hits). The sites recording the most visits as at the end of 2007 in absolute terms were T-Online Content, MSN and Yahoo, followed by the student platform StudiVZ.

The most appealing TV stations

The public-network ARD and ZDF channels compete with the private stations (by market share)

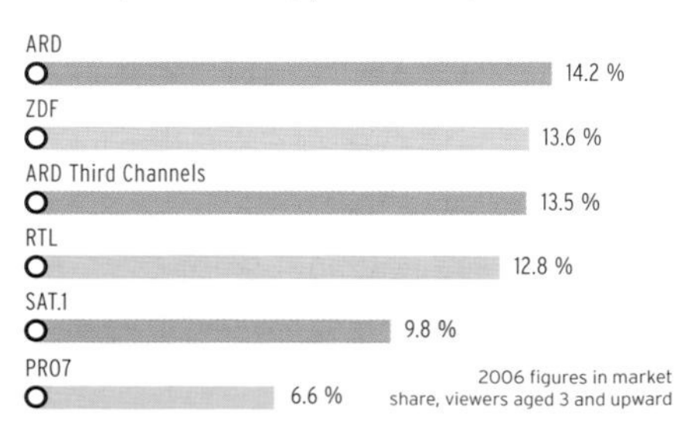

Internet domain registrations

After ".com" ".de" is the most popular top-level domain. ".net" sees 10.4 m, ".org" 6.1 m and ".info" 5.0 m registrations

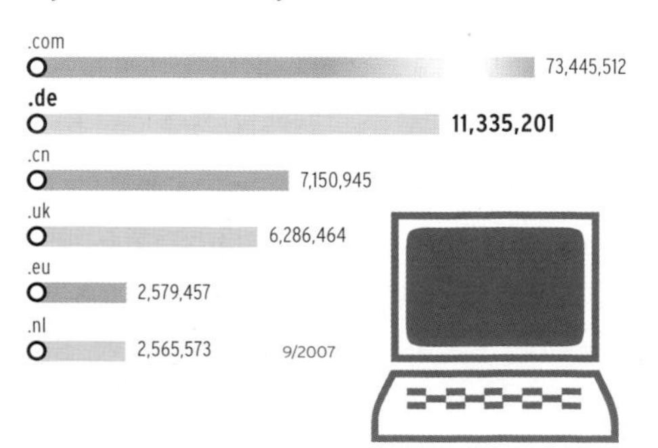

Public and private stations
In Germany, there are in principle two different forms of TV and radio as well as of financing for them. The private stations exist almost exclusively from ad billings – the public stations are financed by license fees and advertising; they are duty-bound to uphold a programming agenda set out in law. There are nine public stations: They are structured by state and all come under the aegis of the ARD, the Arbeitsgemeinschaft der Rundfunkanstalten in Deutschland. Together, they are responsible for programming by Erstes Deutsche Fernsehen (Das Erste), but also broadcast their own TV and radio programs. ZDF is another public station, but it offers no regional programming and is only a TV station.

The customary professional press and radio products still tend to constitute the lion's share of media content. Yet above all the younger generation is increasingly using community communication, such as blogs, as an alternative information source alongside the traditional media. As at the end of 2007, according to the German "Blogcharts", the most frequently linked blogs in Germany include Basicthinking.de, bildblog.de (which focuses critically on the newspaper "Bild") and spreeblick.com. Today, the majority of active blog-users states that these sources are more credible they believe than the usual journalism. The result: In many German media houses forms of products are arising that combine in a new unit the customary work of editors, with its strong craftsmanship and sense of trust, with so-called user-generated content. Thus, in the best case, German media's professional standards are upheld and married to the "democratic" and spontaneous elements of media products created by the public itself. Under the heading of "Digital Germany", not only the communications scene is changing, but political participation, culture and the country's digitalization-driven economy are being linked ever more closely to current international trends.

Broadcasting

Radio and television also play their part in the overall reach of the German media. Having begun in the 1920s

The topic on the Internet

www.dw-world.de
Online service of the German international broadcaster with up-to-date news in 30 languages

www.kulturportal.de
Database run by the Federal Government's Commissioner for Culture with info on events, institutions and persons from the worlds of art and culture (German)

www.litrix.de
Information portal for the worldwide dissemination of contemporary German literature (English, German, Chinese, Arabic, Portugese)

www.filmportal.de
Main Internet platform for information about German films and film makers (English, German)

www.kulturstiftung-des-bundes.de
Web site of the Federal Cultural Foundation with detailed information about project sponsorship (English, German)

www.museen.de
Profiles and addresses of several museums in German-speaking countries as well as dates of current exhibitions; in-depth search function (German)

(radio) and the 1950s (television) as public network institutions, since the 1980s the colorful spectrum of a dual system made up of **public** network channels and **private stations** has emerged. Nowadays some 460 radio stations, for the most part local and regional in character, compete with each other. Some 75 public network radio stations vie with around 385 commercial stations. Overall, in its history radio has undergone a change of function. After the introduction of television it tended to develop more as a parallel medium, and in terms of listening hours achieves about the same figures as TV.

There are differences in the television structure on two levels, national and regional, and between general and special interest channels. Germany has some of the largest public (ARD and ZDF) and private (RTL, Sat1, ProSieben) broadcasting houses in Europe and the world. Depending on the technical platform (terrestrial, satellite, cable, broadband, mobile), and on whether reception is analogue or digital, more than 20 different public TV channels can be viewed, including the two national channels ARD and ZDF, as well as regionally produced offerings broadcast nationwide, such as WDR, MDR, BR and special interest channels like docu-channel Phoenix and kid's TV KIKA. Then there are three international broadcasters: Deutsche Welle, Franco-German arte, and Austro-German-Swiss cultural channel 3sat. The digital strategy pursued by ARD and ZDF also endeavors to provide a TV media library available round-the-clock and new online and mobile products. Here, there is a constant threat of conflict with the private channels, who fear competition will be distorted by the strong influence in the market of the "subsidized" stations. ●

"Deutsche Welle" (DW), which is part of ARD, is responsible for broadcasts abroad. Its mission is to paint a wide-ranging portrait of German political, cultural and economic life, and to present and outline the German angle on key issues

Jo Groebel
A media expert, Prof. Groebel is Director of the German Digital Institute in Berlin; he also teaches communication science at the University of Amsterdam.

11

Modern life

What makes everyday life worth living? Great cuisine and fine wines, relaxing in Mother Nature, festivals and celebrations, vacation, design and fashion, inspiring architecture. Germany has plenty of all to offer - and is far removed from all the clichés that might still abound about lederhosen and sauerkraut. But then the numerous visitors from abroad who are increasingly discovering that Germany is an interesting vacation destination already know this. Not just because of the wealth of German cultural and historical sights, but also because of the wide-ranging regional cuisine and the changing landscapes. In fact, although the Germans are the undisputed world champions when it comes to foreign travel, they still prefer to holiday between the North Sea and the Alps.

Enjoyment and celebrations, travel and living – everyday culture and way of life

By Constanze Kleis

"COSMOPOLITAN AND HOSPITABLE" – this was the laudable label guests at World Cup 2006 gave Germany. According to a poll by TNS Infratest, which was commissioned by Deutsche Zentrale für Tourismus, Germany and the Germans were definitely rated favorably by travelers. And there is no lack of reasons for this positive appeal: the country's modern approach, its openness, the quality of life, the multinational diversity and the creativity with which Germany both renews and preserves its cultural identity. Nowadays a relaxed laissez-faire attitude and a liberal sense of curiosity are evident in almost all aspects of life.

For example in nutrition. Of course you can still enjoy heavy regional cuisine, the hearty characteristics of the different landscapes: Roast pork with dumplings from Bavaria or ribs and sauerkraut from Hesse. Yet several new influences have also made their mark on **German cuisine**. It has become far more varied and health conscious, light and imaginative. In the 2008 edition of Gault Millau, Klaus Erfort from "Gästehaus Erfort" in Saarbrücken was voted "Cook of the Year". His strong suits include "Paté de foie gras in a wafer-thin peppered pineapple crust". Nowadays, that too is typically German cuisine – because the country is developing more and more into a "World Taste Center".

In fact, the Germans are among those with the most international range of food in Europe. According to a survey conducted by the Allensbach Institute more than fifty per-

German cuisine
There is no such thing as standard "German cuisine", rather several regional specialties ranging from smoked sprats from Kiel to white sausage with sweet mustard from Munich. Regional cuisine is also very important for Germany's top chefs. In 2008 Michelin Guide awarded more than 200 German restaurants one or more of its coveted stars. The highest concentration of Michelin stars is in the Black forest community of Baiersbronn. Among Germany's top chefs are Heinz Winkler (Aschau), Harald Wohlfahrt (Baiersbronn) and Dieter Müller (Bergisch Gladbach).

Organic food
Organic agriculture is becoming ever more popular among German farmers. Between 1996 and 2007, the number of farms working according to organic criteria soared from 7,353 to 17,557. More than 40,000 products on sale in German supermarkets and health food shops bear the state organic seal for goods produced organically. There are strict criteria governing the classification "organic": Foodstuffs may not be treated with chemical pesticides or be genetically modified and may only be produced from animals that have been kept in an appropriate manner.

cent of all Germans chose foreign cuisine when eating out, primarily Italian, Chinese or Greek.

Another trend is towards healthy eating: In 2006, sales of **organic food** totaled some 4.6 billion Euro. Organic supermarkets are opening up in large cities all over the country, offering a blend of what is becoming increasingly important to Germans: Enjoyment and responsibility, lifestyle and a clear conscience. At year-end 2006, there were a good 350 organic supermarkets in Germany – 50 more than the prior year.

Less beer, more water

The European Parliament recognizes beer from Germany as being a "traditional foodstuff", a label only awarded to a very few forms of nourishment. This is thanks to the famous "Purity Law" that only allows the use of certain natural ingredients in beer. This means that even today the basics of all German beers are hops, malt, water and yeast. In addition to large breweries, smaller traditional regional breweries have a place in the hearts of beer drinkers. These make up 80 percent of the adult population in Germany. They can chose between 5,000 different brands produced by 1,284 breweries: a world record.

A healthy trend drink: Mineral water gushes from 223 German sources

Nonetheless, beer consumption in Germany is dwindling all the time, from 133 liters a year in 1994 to just 112 liters per person today.

On the other hand, the wellness boom has triggered a bubble in, among other things, mineral water. Over the last 30 years the Germans have increased the amount of mineral water they drink by a factor of ten to 132 liters each, putting them in the top group worldwide. More than 500 types of mineral water gush from 223 sources.

The Riesling miracle

Since the beginning of the new millennium German Riesling wine has been enjoying a Renaissance – on the international stage as well. The world over, it is now a standard item in many top restaurants. In just four years the USA has doubled the amount it imports. Riesling has earned the enthusiasm of wine experts for the "German wine miracle" thanks to its lightness and sparkling character, characteristics that are the result of the particular climatic conditions and soil: because the German wine-growing regions are among the most northerly in the world.

The long period of vegetation and moderate temperatures in summer **make wines from Germany** filigree and keep their alcohol content low. Different soil types and vines such as Müller-Thurgau and Silvaner also play their part in giving German wines a reputation for being remarkably varied.

However, the new generation of vintners in the 13 **German wine-growing regions** has also played its part in the success story, concentrating as it has done on quality rather than quantity. Germany, traditionally a white wine country – of the wine produced in Germany 65 percent is white and 35 percent red –, is increasingly discovering red wine.

The acreage used for cultivation, primarily for Spätburgunder, has already more than tripled. Could this be the next wine miracle?

Wines from Germany

German wines are produced in 13 wine-growing areas in which around 65,000 vineyards produce a wide variety of typical regional wines. Apart from Saxony and Saale-Unstrut in the East, the German wine-growing areas are concentrated in the southwest and south of the country. Although almost 140 types of vine are planted, only two dozen, primarily the white wines Riesling and Müller-Thurgau, have any real market significance.
Of the wine produced in Germany 65 percent is white and 35 percent red. About a quarter of the nine million hectoliters produced annually is exported, in particular to the USA, Great Britain and the Netherlands.

German wine-growing regions

- Ahr
- Baden
- Franconia
- Hessische Bergstrasse
- Mittelrhein
- Mosel-Saar-Ruwer
- Nahe
- Pfalz
- Rheingau
- Rheinhessen
- Saale-Unstrut
- Saxony
- Württemberg

The German National Tourist Board
The German National Tourist Board is headquartered in Frankfurt/Main. Its 29 sales offices, eleven of which are representative offices, and 18 sales cooperation outlets, plan, coordinate and realize its marketing and sales activities abroad.

Hustle and bustle: Over six million peoplefrom all over the world visit the Oktoberfest in Munich every year

Destination Germany

Germany is becoming increasingly popular as a travel destination: With almost 55 million overnights by foreign guests in 2007, the **German National Tourist Board** recorded a notable 3-percent increase on the record achieved during 2006, the World Cup year. Berlin, Munich, Frankfurt and Cologne are the most popular cities with international visitors. Most come from other European countries, the USA and Asia. With regard to individual states, Bavaria, North Rhine-Westphalia and Baden-Württemberg are the preferred destinations.

In addition to historical sights, top-quality concert series, art exhibitions, theater performances as well as major international sports events, not to mention street festivals and atmospheric Christmas markets are just a few of the attractions that bring the visitors flocking. The Germans love to celebrate, and never miss an opportunity to do so. Many festivals such as Munich's renowned Oktoberfest, Christo-

Wellness Holidays

Feel-good Germany: Wellness and health have for years been the rage among tourists. The German Tourism Study 2007 showed that 69 percent of German holidaymakers would most prefer a relaxation and wellness vacation. And an increasing number of foreign guests choose a relaxing holiday in one of the 330 recognized German spa towns and thermal springs. Be it classical massage or Qigong, Chinese energy motion therapy, there are any number of hotels up and down the country specialized in offering wellness holidays. Especially popular are the long-standing sea spa towns along the Baltic coast, such as Heiligendamm (photo), the oldest and perhaps most refined German sea spa town, with a grand hotel that was voted Europe's best beach hotel in 2007. Heiligendamm, the "white town on the coast", is also considered a gesamtkunstwerk of Classicist architecture. South Germany scores highest with a wholesome climate, thermal springs, and "hay baths": Baden-Baden in Baden-Württemberg and Bavaria's Allgäu region are the preferred wellness destinations. And a few insiders know that with 32 therapeutic spa towns, Hesse in the heart of Germany is the country's "no. 1 spa state".

pher Street Day in Cologne, the Carnival of the Cultures in Berlin, Fastnacht in Mainz and Carnival in Cologne have long become an international synonym for high spirits and a cosmopolitan atmosphere.

Whereas most foreign visitors are drawn to the big cities, Germans themselves tend to visit smaller places and rural regions in their home country: The coasts of the North and Baltic Seas, the Black Forest and Lake Constance are the most popular vacation destinations. Germany boasts no less than 14 **national parks**, 95 nature parks and 13 biosphere reserves. However, coastlines, lakes, as well as low and high mountain ranges are all becoming increasingly important as a sort of open-air health club. There are all sorts of opportunities available: There are as many as nine long distance trails stretching for 9,700 kilometers throughout the country and a total of 190,000 kilometers of signposted walks. And for cyclists there are 50,000 kilometers of track on which to discover the country.

National parks
To a large extent the 14 national parks in Germany are located in the north of the country. They are all noteworthy for their unique nature and landscape and serve to preserve the natural diversity of rare plants and animals. The largest is the Schleswig-Holstein Mud Flats National Park Wattenmeer, with a surface area of 441,000 hectares. The smallest, Jasmund National Park on the Isle of Rügen, with its famous white cliffs, is only 3,003 hectares large.

In fine shape – fashion and design

High fashion made in Germany is a firm feature on the international catwalks. For decades now designers such as Escada and Wolfgang Joop have been global players, the latter having recently enjoyed tremendous success with his glamorous new "Wunderkind Couture" label. Not infrequently the big galas and balls in Berlin, Frankfurt and Munich appear to be a showcase for the achievements of German fashion-makers: On show are Escada, Unrath & Strano, Talbot Runhof and Anna von Griesheim – who are popular not just with German high society. In everyday life, Germans tend to focus more on the down-to-earth. In addition to functional business attire they tend to prefer casual sportswear, such as Boss and Strenesse. Though headquartered in southern Germany, both labels have long been well established in international markets.

In major German cities in particular there is ample opportunity for experimenting with fashion.

New creations by the star designer: Wolfgang Joop is causing a stir with his "Wunderkind" label

Design and architecture

Clarity and functionality are still considered to be the fundamental principles of typical German design and architecture. Nowadays, charm and finesse also contribute to "good form"

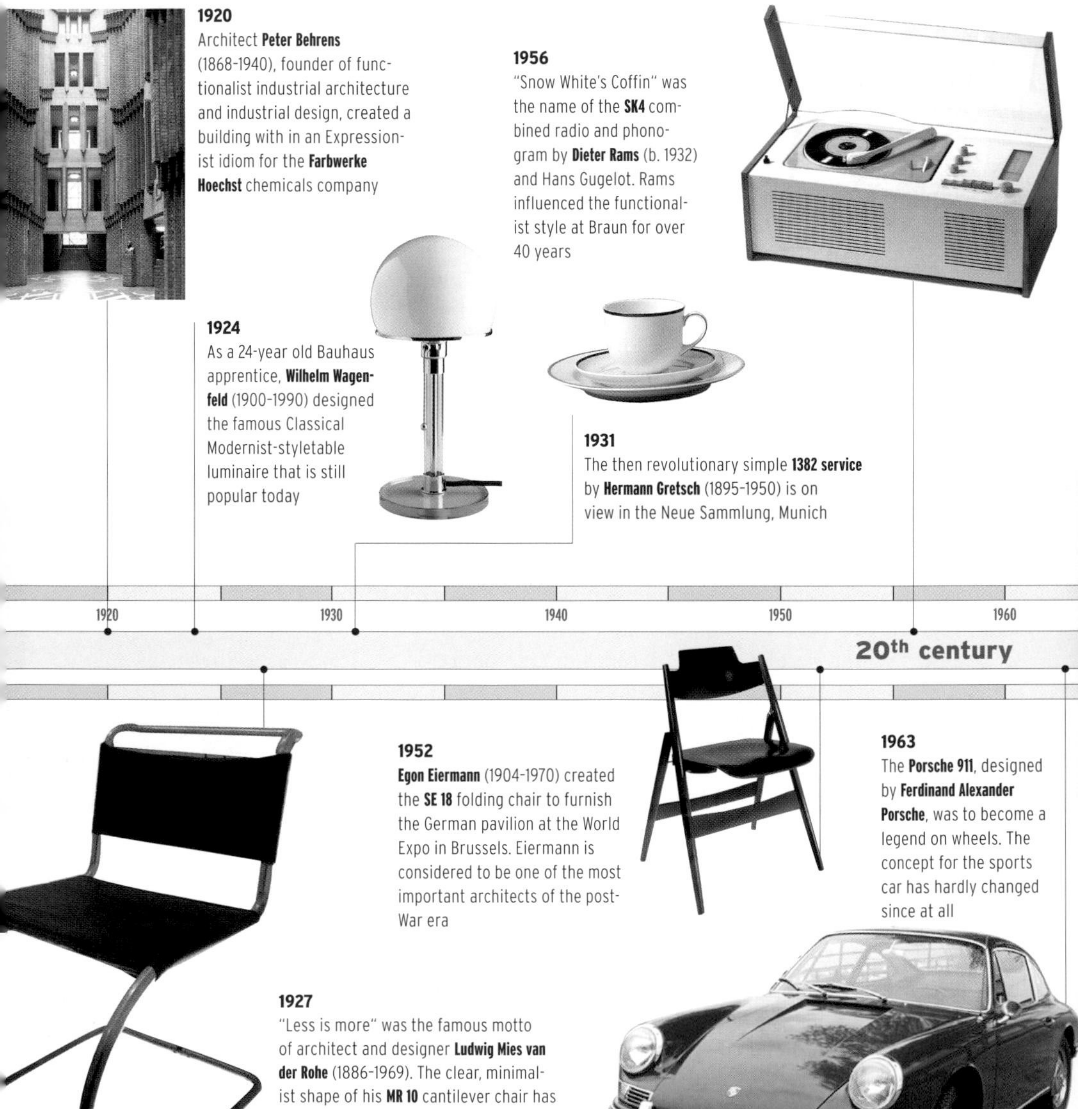

1920
Architect **Peter Behrens** (1868-1940), founder of functionalist industrial architecture and industrial design, created a building with in an Expressionist idiom for the **Farbwerke Hoechst** chemicals company

1956
"Snow White's Coffin" was the name of the **SK4** combined radio and phonogram by **Dieter Rams** (b. 1932) and Hans Gugelot. Rams influenced the functionalist style at Braun for over 40 years

1924
As a 24-year old Bauhaus apprentice, **Wilhelm Wagenfeld** (1900-1990) designed the famous Classical Modernist-styletable luminaire that is still popular today

1931
The then revolutionary simple **1382 service** by **Hermann Gretsch** (1895-1950) is on view in the Neue Sammlung, Munich

1952
Egon Eiermann (1904-1970) created the **SE 18** folding chair to furnish the German pavilion at the World Expo in Brussels. Eiermann is considered to be one of the most important architects of the post-War era

1963
The **Porsche 911**, designed by **Ferdinand Alexander Porsche**, was to become a legend on wheels. The concept for the sports car has hardly changed since at all

1927
"Less is more" was the famous motto of architect and designer **Ludwig Mies van der Rohe** (1886-1969). The clear, minimalist shape of his **MR 10** cantilever chair has lost nothing of its Modernist feel

1972
Richard Sapper was born in 1932 in Munich. One of his most famous objects is the **Tizio** halogen luminaire. He deliberately opted for a formal idiom that oscillates between the playful and the functional

1984
The square is the trademark and leitmotif of several buildings by **O. M. Ungers** (b. 1926). The **Torhaus** at the trade fair grounds in Frankfurt/ Main is a striking example of his unmistakable style, which cuts across all fashions and schools

2007
The **Berlin Fashion Week**, with fashion shows beneath the Brandenburg Gate, is a new key date in global fashion diaries

2003
Konstantin Grcic, who was born in 1965 in Munich, is one of the most successful young designers. **Chair One** is a typical example of minimalist design

1970 1980 1990 2000 2010

21st century

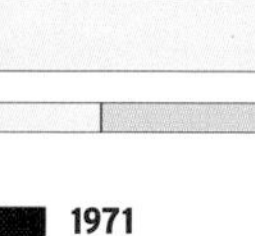

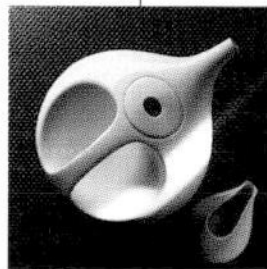

1971
There is hardly any product at which Berlin-born **Luigi Colani** (b. 1928) has not tried his hand. The Drop tea service bears witness to his typically organic shapes

The 1980s and 1990s
Born in 1943, at the height of her success, haute couturier **Jil Sander's** style was clean-lined and elegant

2000
With its unusual pavilion roof, the **Sony Center** at Potsdamer Platz, designed by **Helmut Jahn** (b. 1940), a US citizen of German descent, has been causing a stir. It has quickly emerged as a new Berlin landmark

2005
For 22 years now **Karl Lagerfeld** (b. 1938) has been the creative mind behind **Chanel**. The Metropolitan Museum of Art in New York is devoting a major exhibition to his work

Bauhaus
Bauhaus (1919–1933) is considered to be the most famous art, design and architecture college of Classic Modernism. Founded by Walter Gropius it was located in Weimar and later in Dessau. Bauhaus artists and architects created a new, clear, contemporary formal language, much of which still exerts an influence today. The most famous representatives of Bauhaus include Ludwig Mies van der Rohe, Lyonel Feininger, Oskar Schlemmer and Sophie Taeuber-Arp.

Full of wit and ingenuity, a whole host of creative fashion designers put up stiff competition with fashion centers such as London and Paris. The Berlin Fashion Week, with shows by well-established and new designers, is a key fashion event in the capital.

Insiders have long been familiar with the new German fashion avant-garde, which include Thatchers, Coration, Sabotage, Kostas Murkudis and Eisdieler from Berlin, as well as Blutsgeschwister from Stuttgart, Anja Gockel from Mainz, and Susanne Bommer from Munich. Young German fashion designers such Markus Lupfer, Bernhard Willhelm and Dirk Schönberger have conquered even London, Paris and the fashion-conscious city of Antwerp. That said, the most famous German couturier abroad is undoubtedly Karl Lagerfeld, who was born in Hamburg and is Creative Director of Chanel, the legendary French haute couture company.

German product design has a reputation for creating carefully devised, straightforward functional products. Design made in Germany – from Bulthaup kitchens to Braun razors – is held in high regard in the international arena. Companies such as furniture manufacturers Wilkhahn and Vitra still lead the way in terms of style, as do Lamy for writing implements and Erco for luminaires. The traditions of **Bauhaus** in the 1920s and the Ulm College in the 1950s are still highly regarded, but in the meantime a new generation has made a name for itself. It includes Konstantin Grcic, who was born in 1965 and is one of the most innovative young designers. Born in Munich, he

The topic on the Internet

www.cma.de
The Central Marketing Association of the German Agricultural Industry has recipes and a cookery encyclopedia ready to go as downloads (German)

www.deutscheweine.de
Info from the German Wine Institute in Mainz about wine-growing areas and types of grape (English, German)

www.germany-tourism.de
The German National Tourist Board provides extensive information about destinations and events in Germany (numerous languages)

www.bahn.de
The Web site of Deutsche Bahn, the German railroad system with lots of information (countless languages)

www.europarc-deutschland.de
Background information and links to the Web sites of all 14 German national parks between the North Sea and the Alps (German)

www.german-design-council.de
The German Design Council is a center of expertise for anything to do with design (English, German)

Spectacular: The Elbe Philharmonic Hall designed by Swiss architects Herzog & de Meuron is the heart of the new Hafencity Hamburg and will be commissioned in 2010

accords totally banal everyday objects an unfamiliar touch of poetry. The newcomers from "Studio Vertijet" in Halle, Steffen Kroll and Kirsten Hoppert, also blend playful and analytical design elements in their work.

Architecture

The architectural scene in Germany has several regional centers, but since reunification it has also certainly focused on Berlin. In the capital, world-class architecture can be experienced at close quarters: Whether Lord Norman Foster, who converted the former Reichstag building into the new German parliament, Renzo Piano, Daniel Libeskind, I. M. Pei or Rem Koolhaas – the list of international architects who have made their mark on the new face of Berlin is long. However, the elite among German master builders such as Helmut Jahn, von Gerkan Marg und Partner, Hans Kollhoff and Josef Paul Kleihues have likewise made a firm contribution to the new capital. In the old harbors of Hamburg and Düsseldorf experiments are being conducted with new formal ideas. And in many cities striking museum buildings have been created by German architects – such as Stephan Braunfels' Pinakothek der Moderne in Munich, Frank O. Gehry's Museum MARTa in Herford, Tadao Ando's Langen Foundation near Neuss and the Leipzig Museum of Fine Arts by Berlin architects Hufnagel Pütz Rafaelian. •

Constanze Kleis
The authoress of several lifestyle books works as a freelance journalist for various German magazines and newspapers.

Picture captions

p.6: Boening/Zenit/laif
p.8: Boening/Zenit/laif (2), akg-images
p.9: Volz/laif, Schapowalow, Karl-Heinz Raach/laif
p.10: picture-alliance/dpa (2), Hensler/laif
p.11: Fechner/laif, Zanettini/laif, Wegner/laif
p.12: Elleringmann/laif, RAPHO/laif, Hughes/laif
p.13: Knop/laif, picture-alliance/ZB
p.14, p.16: Westrich/laif
p.17: Stuttgart Marketing GmbH,
TANNER WERBUNG Touristik Kommunikation
p.18: Zielske H.D./laif, Thorsten Krüger
p.19: Archiv der BIS Bremerhaven Touristik,
Zielske H.D./laif, Boening/Zenit/laif
p.20: Zielske H.D./laif (2)
p.21: Zielske H.D./laif, Eisermann/laif
p.24: Ralf Kreuels/laif, DWT/Dittrich,
picture-alliance/dpa
p.25: Celentano/laif
p.26, p.28, p.29: Bundesbildstelle
p.30: ullstein - Archiv Gerstenberg
p.31: akg-images, picture-alliance/dpa
p.32, p.33, S34, p.35: akg-images
p.36: Thorsten Krüger, picture-alliance/akg-images/Erich Lessing, Gutenbergmuseum,
picture-alliance/dpa
p.37: picture-alliance/akg-images/Erich Lessing (2),
akg-images (5)
p.38: Ian Haskell, picture-alliance/obs,
picture-alliance/dpa, akg-images (3),
ullstein - Archiv Gerstenberg
p.39: picture-alliance/dpa (2), photothek,
picture-alliance/ZB, akg-images, CARO/Kaiser
p.40, p.41: picture-alliance/dpa
p.42: Adenis/GAFF/laif
p.43, p.44, p.45: akg-images
p.46, p.47: Bundesbildstelle
p.48: Staubach/artur
p.49: picture-alliance/ZB
p.50, p.52: Boening/Zenit/laif
p.53: picture-alliance/akg-images
p.54: Ralf Hillebrand
p.56, p.57: picture-alliance/dpa/dpaweb
p.58: picture-alliance/dpa, Ralf Hillebrand
p.59: picture-alliance/dpa,
p.60: Teamwork
p.62: picture-alliance/dpa
p.63: Langrock/Zenit/laif
p.64: Boening/Zenit/laif
p.65: CARO/Ruffer
p.66: Bundesrat
p.67: KEYSTONE, picture-alliance/dpa
p.68: picture-alliance/dpa
p.70, p.72: Pierre Adenis/GAFF/laif
p.73: picture-alliance/dpa
p.74: picture-alliance/dpa
p.75: picture-alliance/dpa,
picture-alliance/dpa/dpaweb
p.76, p.78: picture-alliance/dpa/dpaweb
p.79: picture-alliance/ZB (2)
p.82: picture-alliance/dpa (4), picture-alliance/Godong, picture-alliance/akg-images
p.83: picture-alliance/akg-images (2),
picture-alliance/dpa (1),
picture-alliance/dpa/dpaweb (1)
p.86: picture-alliance/dpa/dpaweb
p.88, p.90: Volkswagen
p.91: Enercon
p.94: picture-alliance/dpa, H.-B.Huber/laif
p.95: Daimler AG, Herzan/laif, Kruell/laif
p.96: AMD
p.97: picture-alliance/dpa/dpaweb
p.98: picture-alliance/ZB
p.99: picture-alliance/ZB (2)
p.100: picture-alliance/Helga Lade GmbH,
picture-alliance/dpa/dpaweb
p.101: IAA, Fraport
p.102: Siemens
p.103: picture-alliance/dpa
p.105: BASF, PPS Digital
p.106, p.108: Bildagentur Waldhaeusl
p.109: Action Press/Jörg Eberl
p.110: Paul Langrock/Zenit/laif
p.111: Soda-Club GmbH
p.113: momentphoto.de/Oliver Killig
p.115: Georg Kumpfmüller
p.116, p.118: Lange/laif
p.119: picture-alliance/ZB
p.120: Universität Heidelberg
p.122: Matthias Kulka
p.123: picture-alliance/dpa
p.124: Bildagentur online, Osram, Mifa AG, Siemens
p.125: Miele, DG-Flugzeugbau, A. Vossberg/VISUM,
mtu-online, Aspirin, Daimler AG,
picture-alliance/akg-images
p.126: pratt-whitney, Fischer, Transrapid
p.127: IBM, www.airbup.com, Andreas Varnhorn,
Daimler AG, picture-alliance/Okapia KG/Ge,
Thyssen-Krupp, Rainer Weisflog
p.128: Held/F1-Online
p.130: picture-alliance/dpa (6),
picture-alliance/akg-images (2),
picture-alliance/akg-images/Bruni Meya,
p.134, p.136: Zuder/laif
p.137: picture-alliance/dpa
p.138: picture-alliance/dpa
p.139: REA/laif
p.140: Huber/laif
p.142: picture-alliance/OKAPIA KG
p.143: Societäts-Verlag/Jörn Roßberg
p.144: REA/laif
p.145: plainpicture/Klammt, A.
p.146: picture-alliance/dpa
p.147: Rodtmann/laif
p.148: picture-alliance/ZB
p.149: Gerster/laif
p.151: KEYSTONE
p.152: picture-alliance/dpa
p.154, p.156: picture-alliance/ZB
p.157: Baatz/laif
p.158: Anna Weise, Frank Zauritz/laif
p.159: picture-alliance/dpa
p.160: picture-alliance/ZB, picture-alliance/dpa (2),
picture-alliance/akg-images/Erich Lessing,
picture-alliance/akg-images, akg-images
p.161: picture-alliance/obs, RAPHO/laif,
picture-alliance/dpa, akg-images (2),
picture-alliance/dpa/dpaweb, Kolvenbach
p.162: Auswärtiges Amt
p.163: picture-alliance/dpa,
picture-alliance/dpa/dpaweb
p.164: picture-alliance/dpa, picture-alliance/ZB
p.165: picture-alliance/dpa
p.166: picture-alliance/dpa, Emi Music Ltd.
p.167: picture-alliance/dpa, Berlinale
p.168: Transit/Wolfgang Zeyen
p.169: Kristina Schäfer
p.170: picture-alliance/dpa/dpaweb
p.171, p.173, p.175: picture-alliance/dpa (2)
p.171, p.173: Sonny Munk Carlsen
p.180: Huber/laif,
picture-alliance/Helga Lade GmbH
p.181: picture-alliance/dpa/Stockfood
p.182: Kirchner/laif, Kempinski Heiligendamm
p.173: picture-alliance/KPA/
Gerken + Ernst, Dan Lecca
p.184: akg-images, G.F.Abele/TV-yesterday,
Tecnolumen GmbH+CoKG, Die Neue
Sammlung/Staatliches Museum für angewandte Kunst/München (Foto: A. Laurenzo),
picture-alliance/dpa, Porsche
p.185: Artemide, ddp, akg-images, Rosenthal AG,
Boening/laif, Schirnhofer/Agentur Focus,
picture-alliance/dpa
p.186: Maecke/GAFF/laif
p.187: picture-alliance/dpa/dpaweb, Jörg Ladwig

Our cordial thanks go the staff of the
Federal Statistical Office Germany and the F.A.Z.-archive for their support.

Index

Index